TWELVE RESOLUTIONS
FOR A HAPPY LIFE

MANTICORE PRESS
WWW.MANTICORE.PRESS

TWELVE RESOLUTIONS FOR A HAPPY LIFE

A Manual of Happiness

ABIR TAHA

To all seekers of happiness.

"And then he saw that Brahman was Joy; for from Joy all beings have come, by Joy they all live, and unto Joy they all return."

– Taittiriya Upanishad

CONTENTS

PREFACE

THE NEW YEAR is usually filled with good will and noble intentions; it is all about firm resolutions, second chances, new beginnings, solemn vows to change, to make things better, in short, to be a better person. Thus, on the eve of 2013, and in the spirit of rebirth and renewal, I resolved to change radically and totally.

I made a simple yet firm decision: I decided to take control of my life. Instead of letting things happen to me, and submitting to the will of a capricious "God in heaven," blind fate, or arbitrary chance, I was henceforth going to *make* things happen *for* me. I decided to be happy. Yes, happy; that was not mere wishful thinking but a serious resolution. I was aiming high, my will was strong and my faith was boundless. I decided: no more worries, no more fear, no more regrets. I saw myself as the captain of my own ship, destiny. Life was hereafter going to be filled with joy and meaning; and it was all up to me to make that happen.

Gone was the inveterate pessimist, the priestess of doom and gloom who only saw the half-empty glass and looked at the world through dark lenses. It was a total metamorphosis:

the new me was now in charge, filled with a wonderful zest for life and unlimited hopes and aspirations. A new horizon had opened up and I was now looking at life from above the clouds, there where the sun perpetually shines.

I decided to change, to become an optimist, a great affirmer of life, a "yes sayer." Happiness would no longer be an elusive dream but a conscious decision that I make, a reality in the here and now.

Therefore, to that end, I made twelve resolutions which I vowed to diligently apply and strive to fulfil during the new year and for the rest of my life; so I hurriedly wrote them down: "Twelve Resolutions for a Happy Life." I vowed that these resolutions would turn my life into a symphony of love and joy. Thrilled with their wisdom and with the magical transformation that they would bring about, my husband Dori suggested that I share them with the world in the form of a book, a manual of happiness.

I have no doubt that these twelve deep yet simple resolutions, if earnestly applied to our daily life, can and will deeply and totally transform our existence, bestowing upon it meaning and purpose, and filling it with joy and fulfilment. I hope the readers will benefit from this manual of happiness and that they, as Mahatma Gandhi said, will be the change that they so eagerly wish for themselves and for the world.

Abir Taha

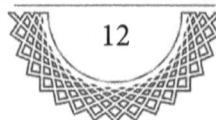

THE QUEST FOR HAPPINESS

"There is no path to happiness. Happiness is the path."
– Buddha

Happiness, An Elusive Dream?

A S HUMAN BEINGS, whatever our race, nationality, culture, or religion, whatever our differences, we all have one thing in common, one fundamental desire, and that is: to be happy. That common basic and simple desire for happiness is the driving force behind our will to live; it is the reason why we wake up every morning filled with hope and faith, ready to grab our share of happiness from Life's many blessings bestowed with grace upon this beautiful green earth.

The quest for happiness is a natural instinct and longing that we all share, whether we speak English, Swahili or Chinese, whether we live in Alaska, in India or in Australia, whether we are Christians, Muslims, Jews, Buddhists, Hindus, or Atheists, whether we are young or old, rich or poor. Of course, we all have our particular dreams and our different goals in life, yet

these dreams and goals all have one thing in common: they are designed and intended to make us feel fulfilled, to give meaning to our lives. And therein lies the essence of happiness.

Each one of us pursues that quest for happiness his own way, the way he thinks will lead him to that desired goal, the way he thinks will achieve that earthly dream of heaven. As there is no theodicy, no universal recipe for happiness, each human being seeks his promised Shangri-la by following a certain path. Thus, some of us seek fortune, others pursue fame, power or glory. Some become obsessed with sex and other addictions; others seek peace and salvation by turning (outwardly) to religion or (inwardly) to meditation. For the romantics among us, life is mainly a quest for love, that blessing from above. And yet, some sceptics, finding no meaning in life, become absolute nihilists who submit to the fact that everything is destined to dissolve once death occurs and shatters all our dreams and aspirations. Still, the rest of us keep on searching for happiness in every which way, hoping to find it and grab a sliver of heaven before we push our last sigh on this earth.

Thus, the whole world keeps pursuing happiness, desperately trying to unveil its secret. All the ideologies and religions promise us their own respective utopias of the "perfect society" and the "perfect man." From East to West, and from North to South, men and women of all ages and from all walks of life are striving to live the Good Life and achieve a prosperous future.

In the developed world, man has built great cities, established huge multinationals, achieved great technological and scientific progress, guaranteeing a life of abundance that is essentially focused on the economy. Indeed, the main goal of the state in the affluent West is providing citizens with a secure life of material comfort and leisure. This way of life has become

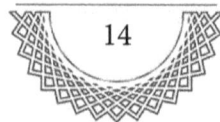

the dominant way of life in modern societies. The "American dream" has become a universal dream, whether one lives in Tokyo, New York, Sao Paulo or Beirut.

And yet, despite investing so much in the pursuit of happiness and abundant life, under the slogan of "life, liberty and property," the West (as well as Westernised societies all over the world) has found peace but *not* happiness, or at least not real, lasting happiness. "Having," not "being," has led to prosperity, comfort and luxury, but it has not given life a meaning. In fact, the West suffers from a crisis of meaning and purpose, since science and technology have not been able to provide the basis of the "Good Life" and the "Good Order" which essentially rests on spiritual and moral elevation and fulfilment.

In the developing world and more traditional societies, people tend to be more conservative and thus they turn to religion in order to find answers and give meaning to their lives. The Easterner tends to be more inclined to meditation and contemplation as a means for attaining happiness. Or so is he *supposed* to be; instead, religious fundamentalism has taken hold of the soul of the East... thus the East specifically the Middle East — suffers from a crisis of reason and freedom. Religion, by preaching salvation and happiness in the "afterlife," has led to the depreciation, and even the negation, of this life.

Thus, both East and West have failed to attain happiness. The life of affluence has only impoverished men's souls, and religion has failed to provide a cure to the ills of society such as poverty, violence and corruption. Wealth has turned man away from religion, and religion has turned man away from God, from his own soul and divine vocation.

And still, we keep pursuing happiness, against all odds and despite life's woes, ills, trials and tribulations. We all pursue happiness, and yet, far from finding it, we instead find ourselves living in a world filled with hatred, violence, war, suffering, competition, greed, crime, etc... On a personal level, we might get close to happiness by leading meaningful, fulfilled lives and by finding love and cherishing friendships, yet we always seem to want more from life, hoping, longing for that blissful state that dreams are made of.

Throughout our lives, we strive to achieve that goal, that promise of eternal bliss, and yet, somehow, happiness eludes us; it remains mankind's collective but unfulfilled dream that haunts us but hardly ever blesses our aching hearts and hollow souls, an ever fleeting shadow of an invisible sun, a shadow that we can never quite catch. And so, all we get are glimpses of joy and love followed by pain, frustration, disappointment and regret. Suffering plagues us from cradle to grave.

We all want to find love and lead successful, meaningful lives, to fulfil ourselves, to realise our full potential. And yet, even with the best will, intention and achievements, we almost never seem to get exactly what we want, or, if and when we do, we still feel dissatisfied; something is still missing, and, despite our deep and constant desire to find happiness, we remain despondent and unfulfilled. In our modern age characterised by greed, hate, violence and deceit, it is hard to find a truly, genuinely happy person, and, if that person actually did exist, he would be a small miracle, an oasis in a desert of desolation. Rich or poor, black or white, young or old, we all seem to share the same dismal fate: suffering. The secret of happiness remains a mystery. So let us delve into the depths of this mystery.

Indeed, before we talk about how to find happiness and why we are unable to find it, we must first try to define — or rather to *redefine* — happiness, since that word has been vulgarised, distorted, and emptied of its real meaning.

Redefining Happiness

Everyone wants to be happy, everyone strives to be happy; but what *is* happiness? What is that state of heavenly bliss which we spend our lives trying to attain, pursuing the fleeting shadow of that invisible sun? We all want to be happy, and yet who really knows what *true* happiness means? We only know that it is a sublime feeling of total bliss that we rarely experience, save during brief moments of evanescent joy experienced throughout our lives, like falling in love, having a mystical experience, getting a big promotion, winning the lottery, etc... and yet true, lasting happiness remains a mirage in the desert of our desolate hearts yearning for wholeness and contentment.

Happiness means different things to different people. Or rather, the means to attain it differ; thus each person pursues the path that he thinks will lead to happiness, according to his nature, character, and his level of spiritual and intellectual awareness. What leads to happiness? Is it love, power, money, fame, glory, the pleasures of the flesh, wisdom, knowledge, religion, agnosticism? There is no one answer to that question, as each person — and how different we all are! — perceives happiness in a different light.

As Plato, that great explorer of the psyche and anatomist of the spirit, discovered thousands of years ago, there are three types of men on the spiritual scale: the instinctive, emotional

and intellectual types. I would describe them respectively as those whose soul dwells in their stomach, those whose soul dwells in their heart, and those whose soul dwells in their head.

The appetitive, instinctual types tend to lean toward that which gratifies the senses. They favour and pursue material comfort and wealth, and physical pleasures like food or sex. The emotional types, those moved by the heart, tend to favour that which intoxicates them, the passion of love or the pursuit of glory through war, or serving a righteous cause, or devoting their lives to helping others. The contemplative, reflective types tend to relish the pursuit of Truth — in itself and for itself — finding happiness in seeking and finding — or even creating — the meaning of life.

These three types of men can be found in all classes, regardless of their material possessions or social status. That is the spiritual hierarchy which reflects the natural hierarchy of the universe. However, these three very different categories of men have one thing in common, and that is: the desire to be happy. They all pursue happiness in their own way.

Thus, the means to attain happiness abound, according to one's nature, one's soul. Indeed, many are the paths that lead to happiness. But what is happiness itself? For without defining true happiness — or rather without *redefining* happiness — how can we pursue it and remove the obstacles that hamper our search for bliss on earth?

So what exactly *is* happiness? I shall venture a comprehensive definition:

Happiness is inner peace, contentment and plenitude which stem from a pacified heart, a purified soul, and a liberated mind.

This is my definition of happiness. Few people would disagree with this definition, for, after all, are we not all in search of absolute unity, absolute peace, absolute love, and absolute freedom? And that is what happiness is: absolute unity of body, mind and spirit, absolute peace which transcends all conflicts, absolute love which blesses life itself, and absolute freedom which breaks all chains and bounds. One word, however, summarises all these absolutes: contentment. *Contentment is the secret of happiness* and the ultimate aim of all mortals.

Contentment is when we feel complete, when we feel whole, as though our souls have expanded and have embraced the whole universe, breaking all the barriers that separate us from all other living creatures. When we are content, there are no limits between us and the world, we have become one with life, with the meaning and purpose of life itself. We feel deep love and reverence for life. We lack nothing, we need nothing. We are sufficient unto ourselves, we have ceased searching and yearning. *Peace, contentment, plenitude: these always go together.*

We are only truly happy when we are content, and we are only truly content when we are truly ourselves. Therefore, be true to yourself, to your nature, to your dreams.

What ensures contentment? Self-fulfilment; realising our full mental, moral, emotional potential. *"Become who you are,"* Nietzsche entreated us. I would add: be the person you *want* to become. The future is now: the fruit is contained in the seed, and the seed in the fruit.

If the key to truth is "know thyself," *the key to happiness is "be thyself."* Self-fulfilment is the path to happiness. This cannot be done without love, which is the essence and the very soul of happiness; love of oneself, love of the others, and love of life.

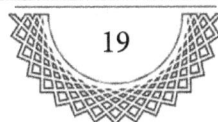

Before we pursue, however, a clear distinction must be made between happiness and what we *think* leads to happiness; indeed, most of us confuse the means with the end, the means to attain happiness and happiness itself, and thus we end up living for the things that we think will make us happy: money, love, sex, power, fame… but eventually we find out that nothing can bring happiness save happiness itself. Happiness is a state of mind that one should desire for its own sake: as the great Buddha said, *"there is no path to happiness. Happiness is the path."*

Another distinction must also be made, before we continue our task of redefining happiness, and that is between pleasure and happiness, between joy and happiness. Pleasure and joy are evanescent, external *moments* of happiness, glimpses of ecstasy, but they are fleeting feelings that soon evaporate and turn into lack and frustration. True happiness is an inner lasting state of mind, not related to outer events, things, or people (although these contribute to happiness but are *not* happiness itself).

True happiness is an inner state, not an outer reality. It is related to how we think and feel. Our surroundings: people, things, events, possessions, wealth, power etc… might contribute to making us happy, but ultimately true happiness comes from within. *The seat of happiness is the soul.* Therefore, purifying our soul and removing the negative thoughts from our mind allows us to become happy.

As we have said above, happiness is essentially a matter of contentment, a state of self-sufficiency, wholeness and inner peace. When we are content, we are sufficient unto ourselves. We are no longer seeking, no longer longing, no longer wanting. Happiness comes from contentment. And contentment comes from self-fulfilment.

Now what brings self-fulfilment? Self-fulfilment is when we become who we are, when we find and attain meaning in our lives, when we achieve our dream, when our thoughts, longings and feelings become realities. Happiness is therefore a state of perfection and wholeness that is only experienced when we know who we truly are and what we came to accomplish down under; in other words, when we find our true nature, meaning and purpose in life and we thus fulfil our duty or path, what the Hindus call *Dharma*. *The soul's fulfilment: that is true and lasting happiness.*

We all have an inner and an outer purpose. The link between our inner and our outer purpose is the same link between our soul and our body: the former shapes the latter and moulds it in its own image. Even as our body is but the reflection of our soul, so too is our outer purpose but the reflection of our inner purpose. Our inner purpose is the nature and purpose of our soul, which only truly unfolds and blossoms when it is expressed and realised in the world, with the others, through our outer purpose which we call "destiny" (in truth, there is no destiny beyond the destiny we choose for ourselves); thus we leave our trace in history. Only thus do we truly live. For if we do not leave a trace — any trace, however small — in history, we have not truly lived.

Each one of us is born for a reason, to fulfil a certain purpose, from the simple peasant who plants the seeds of life to the rocket scientist who seeks to discover the origin of the universe; from the factory worker who weaves the clothes we wear to the philosopher who feeds our minds and the composer who enchants our souls... we are all here for a reason, and we have not lived if we have not fulfilled our purpose on this earth. *To truly live is to create.* Life is eternal creation and nothing else.

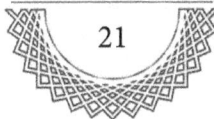

Those who truly live are co-creators in the eternal dance of the cosmos.

Why Are We Unhappy?

If today we walk the streets of any big city, whether in the developing or developed world, we need only look at people's empty stares, sombre countenances and gloomy moods to ask ourselves: why aren't we happy? What is lacking in our lives? Happiness is a collective dream that remains a mirage... we never seem to find the contentment, peace and lasting joy that would make our lives worth living. Of course, we all experience rare moments of joy, but most of the time something is missing, something lacks for us to feel totally happy and content.

Countless religions, ideologies, philosophies, theories, prophets, saints, politicians, etc... have tried — and continue to try — to "save" man from his dismal plight, and yet mankind remains the same, plagued with violence, greed, envy, hate, fanaticism, vice, selfishness... why all this misery? What is it which prevents us from finding true and lasting happiness in our lives?

Why aren't we happy? I am not talking about those brief moments, glimpses of joy that we experience from time to time; what I am talking about is genuine, lasting happiness, the happiness that comes from a feeling of plenitude and fulfilment. Why is happiness a dream, a wish, a longing, but never a reality? Why can't we find happiness now, in the here and now, not merely in a nostalgic dream of a distant and dead past, or a desperate hope for a better future that never comes?

We have seen above that true happiness is self-fulfilment, fulfilling our purpose in life. It is discovering, believing in, and pursuing our dreams. Until we do so, we are not truly living. Meaning is what makes life worth living. *Finding meaning in or giving meaning to life is the secret of happiness.*

Thus, unhappiness is when we do not know what our life purpose is, for what reason we were born; or when we do know what our purpose is but we stray away from our path and pursue other goals that have little to do with our nature and destiny, our *Dharma*. Thus we feel incomplete, unfulfilled, and separated from our destiny and ourselves. And no amount of possessions, power, fame or glory can bring us true and lasting happiness, for *happiness lies not in what we have but in what we are.* The bliss of the soul can only be experienced from within. Our outer purpose is essentially dictated by our inner purpose and nature.

The quest for happiness is ultimately a quest for wholeness. Only by being whole do we feel happy. But to do so we must adopt a set of conduct and rules that will let us live this wholeness, live in harmony with ourselves and the world.

Happiness, A Conscious Decision

Are we doomed to suffer throughout our lives? Is suffering our *only* fate? Our eternal curse down under? No mortal can escape suffering; that is the law that rules the finite world of mortals. Death, illness, old age, will always plague our lives. There will always be injustice, violence, hatred, envy, greed in our imperfect world. However, we might ask ourselves: can't we

also make the best out of life, enjoying its many wonders and joys and finding meaning in it?

The Buddhists preach the annihilation of the ego — which is characterised by desire and fear, source of all our woes — as the only way to avoid suffering and to find happiness. Yet, I argue, this is unnatural, unhealthy, unrealistic and impossible. It is tantamount to moral suicide, for the ego is an integral part of our being; it is the divine, eternal soul's human, mortal twin. And yet the soul is — and should remain — primary. Indeed, while our ego serves our outer purpose and thus leads to outer happiness or rather to pleasure, our soul is the essence of our inner purpose which leads to inner happiness, the only true happiness.

The goal, therefore, is not to deny our ego but to control it and use it as a vehicle for creation and self-fulfilment; not to banish desire but to sublimate it; not to deny life but to live it abundantly. Buddhism is a noble religion of compassion and detachment; and yet, pushed to its extreme, it leads to spiritual self-annihilation, to nihilism, life negation. It would be tantamount to throwing the baby along with the bath water.

Nirvana — total liberation — has been erroneously equated with self-denial and life-negation. Detachment is not death but rather true freedom, freedom from earthly attachments and the prison of matter; this freedom is the essence of a higher life. The truth is that the ego is but an instrument that could lead either to the elevation or to the deterioration of the soul, depending on how we choose to use it, on whether we use it as a means to an end (self-consciousness), or as an end in itself (selfish materialism or hedonism).

By totally abolishing desire, we would also abolish ourselves, or at least an important part of ourselves. Indeed, the many joys

of life are a blessing that is supposed to be lived, not denied. The goal, therefore, is to *live* life, not escape it by denying it and denying our own nature. The goal is not self-annihilation but self-mastery, self-overcoming and elevation; not life denial but life affirmation. With practice and will, the ego can be turned from the cause of all suffering into an instrument for self-fulfilment. Thus it will be in the service of life, an affirmation of life.

Thus, ultimately, when we ask ourselves the eternal question: why are we unhappy? The answer is quite simple and boils down to this: it is because we have forgotten that *happiness is first and foremost an attitude*, an attitude towards ourselves, towards others and towards life.

True happiness, far from being an unreachable ideal, a fantasy, is a conscious decision, a daily practice, a set of natural reflexes that we have unlearned throughout the ages; a lost simplicity that we have eradicated from our lives because of our wrong beliefs and behaviour. *Happiness is a conscious decision* made every single moment of every single day. Happiness is a state of mind, not an elusive dream. It is a daily practice.

Happiness needn't remain a mirage on earth. All it takes is to define or rather redefine it so that it becomes not a mere wish but a real possibility. This book shows the path that leads away from unhappiness toward a meaningful life that is in accordance with our true nature and vocation. It is then up to each reader to find his own path to happiness according to his own nature, purpose and destiny. Heaven thus becomes within reach, an inner state of peace and a deep sense of fulfilment.

So what does this book promise? Is it yet another empty promise of finding an ever elusive happiness? This book promises no such thing. What it does is first explain *why* we're

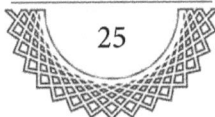

unhappy, what is lacking for us to feel fulfilled and contented, and it then shows us how to get rid of the false and negative concepts, fears and thoughts that are the underlying causes of our unhappiness.

By doing so, it shows us how to remove the obstacles and the wrong thinking and behaviours that hamper our quest for happiness. It then teaches us to focus on finding our true nature, and thus our true purpose in life. When we live in accordance with nature, with our real nature, when we connect with our souls and pursue the destiny that is engraved in our innermost being, we discover our true vocation in life and we become aligned with our purpose and destiny and thus feel contentment. And from contentment springs peace and happiness.

The twelve resolutions that I now share will help the readers to adopt the right attitude towards themselves, towards life, and towards the others at every moment of every day. Thus happiness becomes a daily practice; it is lived as a reality and not just a wish or an ideal. *Heaven becomes possible on earth, in the here and now.*

FIRST RESOLUTION

I Shall Not Hate

"La haine, c'est l'hiver du cœur."[1]

– Victor Hugo

HATE IS A powerful, negative emotion which has disastrous consequences on our mental, moral and psychological well-being and on the well-being of society as a whole. Some would ask, why did I not rather choose to say "I shall *love*" instead of "I shall not *hate*"? Love is a positive emotion; love is superior to the mere absence of hatred. If hatred is human, love is divine. So why not talk about love instead? That would seem more logical and more appropriate, and certainly more romantic, wouldn't it? Especially since everyone seems to love Love. Yet, I argue, granted that love is preferable and superior to the mere absence of hatred, it is also more idealistic and hence less realisable.

More often than not, love is a collective fantasy that remains mere wishful thinking. We all *want* to love, but few of us actually *do*. *"All you need is love,"* goes the famous Beatles song, and yet love is rarely what we give and receive, especially at the collective level. Beyond the narrow love for our sweetheart, close family and friends, most of us seem to be oblivious to the well-being and happiness of society, let alone mankind as a whole.

The sorry state of the world we live in today is a clear proof and a painful and constant reminder that hatred is more widespread than love. It therefore follows that we should strive

---

[1] *"Hatred is the winter of the soul."*

to eradicate the scourge of hatred from our hearts, before we can be able to truly love. That is why I chose to say "I shall not hate" instead of "I shall love."

Indeed, before one can love, before one can truly and fully love life and his fellow man, one must first purify oneself from hatred. And *that* is easier said than done, for we hate so many things — and people — in life, and half the time we are not even conscious of this insidious, silent hatred that consumes our souls and poisons our lives and relationships. That pernicious feeling often lies dormant in our hearts but nonetheless impairs our judgement and spoils our relationship with the world.

Of course, we deny that, we would like to think that we are kind, loving beings; but the truth is that there is some hidden hatred, wickedness, bias, or prejudice in each one of us common mortals which becomes a natural reflex, a second nature in us and prevents us from experiencing, giving and receiving love.

Therefore, we must purify our soul from the hatred that plagues it; we must get rid of our conscious and unconscious hatred before we can be blessed with the divine light of love. Otherwise, the desire and the call for universal love to prevail would remain a utopia; an unrealistic, impossible fantasy. And, alas! It is and remains so...

It is truly paradoxical and sad how everyone wants love, and yet love is so hard to find down under; it remains a hope and a promise, mankind's ever fleeting dream. The truth, the hard fact that we should face and deal with, is the realisation that we must end hatred before we can love.

When the heart is purified, then love comes naturally and fills our soul with its blessed presence. Where hatred ends, there love begins. *Only the soul that is purified can love. The soul that is purified can only love.*

Hatred is the evil of our time. It is — alas! — omnipresent in our day and age. Let us stop burying our heads in the sand and start acknowledging the sad reality: the world we live in is filled with hatred. One need only watch the news to see how dark our world is: crime, violence, wars, massacres, atrocities, fanaticism... There is no room for love in such a world ruled by lust for power, greed and cruelty. Hatred plagues our whole planet. The Hindus describe our age as the *Kali Yuga*, the Dark Age. It is hard to argue with that description, that is, if we want to face the hard and terrible reality and try to change it.

"You are what you think," say the Hindus and Buddhists: our thoughts shape our reality. The outer is a reflection of the inner; the social is a reflection of the personal. ***Our society is a reflection of our souls.*** Thus, at the personal level, we do not fare well either, though we may think we are "good people." The truth is, if we observe ourselves, if we observe our thoughts as a silent, objective witness, we would be shocked to find out how much hatred and prejudice — often surreptitious and unconscious — our minds are filled with. But this hatred has become such a natural reflex that we do not even think about it as being "bad." It is just "being human"... We hate so many things and so many people, most of the time without even consciously realising it. We common mortals spend most of our time being annoyed by little things, instead of appreciating the joy of being and life's many blessings.

Throughout the day, faced with life's many trials and tribulations, we develop negative feelings; it is us against the world which we generally perceive as being hostile and cruel. And this negativity goes on every day of our lives. Finally, on our deathbed, we realise with sorrow and regret that we have hated much more than we have loved, that we have hated

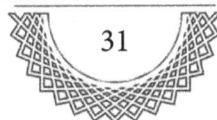

much and loved little, and that we have wasted our life looking at it from the perspective of hate, not of love... the fact is that we are prisoners of our egos which are plagued with greed and fear, which in turn breed conflict and hatred. It is the *war of all against all,"* a Hobbesian nightmare where atomistic egos compete for power and domination. The result is constant tension and confrontation between men; it is "us" against "them" and me against the world. That is the sorry state of our earth.

Why, are we compelled to ask, is there so much hatred in the world and in our souls? The answer is simple: difference. No two people are the same on this planet. Each man is unique, differentiated from even his closest relatives by virtue of possessing a unique soul and character. Our uniqueness is a blessing, but it can also be a problem or even a curse. Indeed, **difference breeds fear.** We feel threatened by what we do not understand. Most of us dislike people, ideas, and things that are different from us. Anything and anyone that does not resemble us breeds fear, mistrust, and sometimes even hatred.

We are ruled by our egos; even if we don't admit it, deep inside, we think *we* are the centre of the universe and all the others should revolve around our sun, should be like us. This illusion — and delusion — creates separation. Thus we do not accept the others; we shun the diversity that characterises life and our earth. Of course, this is an unnatural instinct since nature itself is diverse; it is full of different creatures, plants, landscapes. There is a fundamental unity of things, the same energy pervades the universe, but this energy is manifested in various ways and forms.

The world is made up of so many different cultures, races, nations, religions, political and ideological creeds and opinions, etc... and yet most of us do not seem to accept that reality; deep

within, we simply and honestly have a hard time accepting the "others," those who lack manners, speak the "wrong" language, worship the "wrong" god or have the "wrong" skin colour. We think that *we* are the ideal, we delude ourselves into believing that the world revolves around us and that everyone else should be like us, should conform to our standards, tastes, and beliefs. We think that we alone are right and that the others are wrong. This kind of arbitrary judgment erects barriers between "us" and the "others."

As long as differences persist, we turn them into identities and erect barriers between us and the others. If others fail to conform to our standards, character, beliefs and world-view, we simply reject or avoid them. With such an attitude, the relationship with the others more often than not becomes conflictive and is always unequal: instead of perceiving others as peers, as fellow human beings, we either feel superior to them, and therefore we only feel contempt for them, we try to dominate or oppress them, or at the very least, ignore them; or we are the ones who feel inferior, and hence we feel envy and resentment or even hatred towards them. Therefore, our relationships are characterised by domination, fear or envy. Hatred thus takes hold of our souls.

Difference gives us a sense of identity. Hence we cling to our differences because they define us. Identities are at the core of our hatred: we belong to a certain race, class, nation, we follow a certain religion and political ideology. We assemble with people who are like us and avoid, fear or hate those who are different. It is the famous "us versus them" syndrome that lies at the heart of conflict and tension between nations and individuals. Of course there will always be an elect, enlightened few who treat the other fellow humans with respect, but, alas, most human

relationships remain conflictive because of the differences and incomprehension separating men.

Another — justified — reason for hatred is when we are the victims of injustice or oppression. Revolution is a legitimate mass reaction to injustice. Yet we should realise that hatred only breeds hatred. It is a vicious circle that perpetuates itself endlessly. Real change can only occur when people's *attitudes* change. Winning the hearts and minds of men and women is thus the real lasting revolution. Gandhi liberated his people and his land from colonialism through *Ahimsa* (non-violence). His exemplary life and death made him join the pantheon of the Immortals. Yet, alas! Such a spiritual Master remains the exception, not the rule, and hatred continues to wreak havoc in the world and in our souls.

What is the impact of all that hatred on us and on the world?

At the personal level, hatred makes us morally, spiritually and psychologically sick; it consumes us, it darkens our soul, hardens our heart and numbs our mind. When we hate, we are not tuned to our natural frequency, which is love, love of life and love of others.

At the social level, hatred breeds division, separation, tension, poisoned and dysfunctional relationships, conflict; we become bitter, isolated, atomistic individuals in hostile, strife-ridden communities. Being unhealthy and unnatural, hatred poisons our life and our relationship with the others. Of course there will always be reasons to hate; therefore, as said above, there is no hope of change or of attaining peace and harmony if we do not change our *attitude* towards the others and towards life.

Hence, we should accept the world as it is: diverse, like the colours of the rainbow which all spring from, and are all united, in white. One can speak of "diversity within unity," and

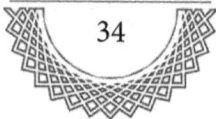

"unity embracing diversity." That is nature in its purest form. *The beauty and richness of this earth lie in its diversity.* That does not mean that we cannot choose our own way of life or mingle with people whom we feel close to or share values with; this of course is a free choice. Rather, it means that we stop hating those who are different from us and view them not as hostile to us but rather as complementing us. The ideal world is a world without hate; a world without hate is a world filled with empathy, peace, and harmony. *Where the ego sees difference and division, the soul sees unity and harmony.*

How to achieve that utopia in the here and now? How to live a hate-free life? How to attain inner peace and stop being consumed by hatred and annoyed by differences? The answer is a simple formula for happiness and peace:

"Live And Let Live."

That famous sentence is frequently and widely used as a way out of hatred, tension and conflict. We should learn from nature, the school of life: lions and hyenas utterly detest each other, but they do not set out to annihilate each other. They co-exist, away from and indifferent to each other. God or Nature — or the Energy that pervades the universe, whatever you want to call the Force behind creation — gave us the gift of life. Therefore, we all have a fundamental human right, the inalienable right to exist: the highest and the lowest among us, the richest and the most destitute, the smartest and the less intellectually endowed among us.

What exists has the right to continue existing. One should not "play God" and decide which life is worthy and which life is unworthy. We are all the sons and daughters of Mother Nature.

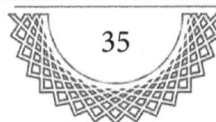

She alone gives and takes life according to her grand scheme and her "mysterious ways."

Every creature — be it an ant, a horse or a man — has the right to exist. Living beings were born to do just that: *live*. We are destined — for better or for worse — to coexist with our fellow human beings and all living creatures under the sun. *Deciding to wipe out a certain creature, a certain species or a certain race is not only immoral but unnatural:* it would be messing with the delicate balance of nature.

All creatures on this earth have a right to exist and to fulfil a certain function, their specific function which is embedded in their genes; in other words, to fulfil their *Dharma* or life purpose. Just as all kinds of creatures characterise the animal world, so too, all kinds of individuals characterise the human world. We learn by looking at nature: in it there is great and rich diversity, and yet also harmony and unity. If we learn to live according to nature, we would embrace and cherish our differences and accept one another as sons and daughters of life.

Live and let live: that is the key to peace and happiness. Be whatever you want to be, but respect the freedom and views of others who, just like you, want to live according to their idiosyncrasies, beliefs, customs, cultures, etc... Free will is a God-given gift and our natural right as the sons of creation. Therefore, develop an objective attitude towards the others, either have compassion for them or, if they really annoy you, just let go.

Having compassion or "letting go": that should be your attitude towards the others. In either case, have tolerance, accept difference as natural and even desirable. Detach yourself from your egotism or egocentrism. Tell yourself you cannot change people, each has his own make-up and his own path. *Be the best version of yourself, an inspiration for others.*

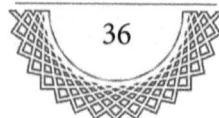

Cherish — or at least respect, accept and tolerate — the differences. You are who you are, unique, different from the others, even from your closest friends or relatives. *Every man is an island;* and yet, for better or for worse, we are condemned to coexist with each other. Therefore, we should build bridges between us, find common ground with others: that is the only way to survive and live in a harmonious, peaceful world. However, our relationship with the others should be genuine, not based on coercion, fear, or mistrust.

Hatred is abolished naturally and intrinsically by accepting difference and respecting and preserving diversity as a natural, essential feature of life and of nature. We are all God's or Nature's creatures, we all have the right to exist. No one can nor should wrest that right away from us; no one should try to eliminate the other. Diversity is richness and creativity. We must perceive the uniqueness of each individual as enrichment of life, and as an experience of self-enrichment. What a boring world would it be if all creatures, human or non-human, were alike! This does not mean that we should give up our own values or stop assembling with people with similar interests or beliefs. But this should be a free choice; again, we should live and let live.

As for those who have harmed or wronged us, or those who have wrought injustice or oppression upon us, we can and should strive to change that by fighting for our rights and our freedom, fighting for the good, the just, and the beautiful, but without being consumed by hatred and only feeling we are doing the right thing following our duty and conscience.

Seeking justice is always a noble cause; yet it should be done without the desire for revenge, because *hatred turns the oppressed into oppressors.* The light should never turn into

darkness lest it become darkness itself. Forgiveness is a noble quality, yet it is seldom practiced and often ignored.

We should therefore forgive those who have harmed us, if not for their sake, at least for the sake of our inner peace. The power of forgiveness is divine; it is healing. We should not seek revenge but justice. Revenge is filled with hatred, whereas justice is imbued with and inspired by love. Thus, when we are hurt by someone, we should overcome our hatred lest we become as wicked as those who have hurt us. Darkness begets darkness, hatred begets hatred. Only love can heal the wounds; hatred only spreads the disease.

If you cannot forgive, if you are the victim of a great injustice, just ignore those who have hurt you. Let go. Life itself will judge them. There is a beautiful Buddhist saying: *"how people treat you is their karma. How you react is yours."* Therefore, act according to your conscience; always do the right thing, against all odds. That is the way to peace and serenity. Have compassion for, or ignore those who have hurt you. Have compassion, forgiveness, or indifference, but do not let hate plague you. Get rid of it; it is a poison that consumes your soul. You would only be hurting yourself. *"The happiest man is he who has no evil in his soul,"* said Plato.

What is the impact of such a positive attitude towards life? If we accept and respect the others with all their differences and peculiarities, we would stop hating, we would become better persons, as hatred makes us and the world around us sick and dark. Thus we coexist in peace and harmony as the Sons of Life.

SECOND RESOLUTION

I Shall Believe

"Faith is the bird that sings when the dawn is still dark."
– Rabindranath Tagore

WHEN I SAY "I shall believe," I am not talking about belief in childish superstitions, in rigid, fixed creeds and narrow dogmas, limited ideas that enslave our minds and stifle our souls. I am rather talking about a higher kind of faith, *faith in the soul, our "luminous twin"*; I am talking about the belief that we are not only made of flesh and bones but that we possess a soul which seeks to fulfil itself by affirming, celebrating and elevating life.

This *enlightened faith* — as opposed to blind faith, dogmatism and fanaticism of any kind — consists in believing in the soul's immortality, believing that there is a higher intelligence or Great Principle governing the universe, that the universe is a Whole and that we are all integral, interconnected parts of this All, of this energy that pervades the entire cosmos and dwells in the unfathomable depths of our souls.

In short, it is a belief in Life itself and its many wonders and mysteries that we should embrace if we want to live life abundantly and to fulfil ourselves and realise our full potential, our destiny on this earth.

Even Nietzsche, the iconoclast and the nihilist who rejected religious beliefs and superstitions, and called himself "the most godless," even Nietzsche had his own belief, his own vision of

divinity, mocking the mediocre, uncreative "realists" as narrow souls "unworthy of belief":

"For thus you speak: 'We are complete realists, and without belief or superstition': thus you thump your chests — alas, even without having chests!... Unworthy of belief: that is what I call you, you realists! ... You are unfruitful: therefore you lack belief. But he who had to create always had his prophetic dreams and star-auguries — and he believed in belief!"

Faith gives meaning to our lives, and gives life to our dreams. Nothing great can be accomplished without faith and the passion that comes with it, without love for a person or an ideal, without an overflowing will to live and an inexhaustible faith in life. What do I mean by "faith" or "belief"? When I say "I shall believe," I mean that I should embrace the thought that there is something that is eternal, divine and indestructible in Man and in Nature; as already stated above, that universal, omnipresent force is the soul, man's immortal soul, which is an integral part of the Soul of the World, otherwise known as ether or *Fohat*, the life-force.

Belief is first and foremost belief in the soul or "breath of God," what the Hindus call *Atman*.

Why is it important — for our spiritual well-being — to believe? To believe in "God," a supra-sensible Force or Principle governing our universe? What is wrong with being — and remaining — an atheist? After all, all things considered, religions have only brought us war, mass murders, superstition, ignorance and bigotry. It is important to note that when I talk about belief, it is *not* in the religious but in the *spiritual* sense. The difference is great. What does that mean?

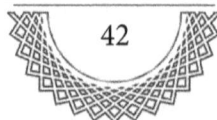

Religions affirm, they offer certainties, crude, simple and even childish answers to philosophy's great questions and life's unfathomable mysteries: "where did we come from? Why do we exist? Where are we going?"

Spirituality, on the other hand, just like philosophy, offers no such simplistic answers to life's ageless questions; rather, it opens our minds and frees our souls by connecting us with the higher Consciousness that governs the cosmos, or what Theosophists call the "I Am That." *Spirituality considers that man is not separate from nature and from God, rather man is a microcosm,* he is intimately linked to the divine that dwells in his very soul. It therefore links our souls with the soul of Nature, which is divinity manifested and eternally evolving. Thus microcosm (man) and macrocosm (the universe, God) merge in the bosom of Being. Spirituality is therefore a way of life, a way to live the perfect life in the here and now, in contrast to the religious promise of an "afterlife" that never comes.

Atheists believe in no God while religious people generally believe in a transcendental, unreachable "God in heaven." Both deny man's higher nature, vocation and destiny, the former by denying the divine altogether, the latter by separating God from his own creation and considering that we mortals are mere servants of this eternally unknowable idol "in the skies." Thus, both atheists and religious people deny life by denying its totality and its higher purpose. In contrast, spirituality — which is the esoteric, eternal essence of all religions — affirms and elevates life, for it believes that God's soul dwells in man, that the human is but a manifestation of the divine on earth, that *man's origin and destiny are divine.*

While philosophy eternally asks questions and religion always "answers" these questions, spirituality, on its part, is

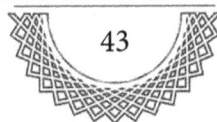

essentially about possibilities, the infinite possibilities that lie between the great questions and their answers. Spirituality is the awe that results from the inexhaustible potentials which stem from creation and eternal becoming. Christ said: *"the Truth shall set you free"*; that, in a nutshell, is the noble aim of spirituality, which is also known as Theosophy (*Theo-Sophia*) or the Wisdom Religion.

The knowledge that the divine permeates the human, and that God and Man are Father and Son, that knowledge, that truth liberates our immortal souls from the chains of the material and transient world, and that liberation occurs in the here and now, not in some distant "heaven."

Real heaven or Nirvana is an inner state of mind. That is the truth which sets us free. That is the higher, enlightened faith that moves mountains, the stuff that miracles are made of. That is what I mean by "I shall believe."

"Does God exist?" That inevitable question, which has haunted humanity since the dawn of existence, perpetuates itself endlessly, with no tangible and convincing answer to this day. It is worth noting that by "God," I do not mean the "God" of religions who is made in man's image — jealous, wrathful, capricious, imperfect — but rather the God who made man in his own image: *"I am searching for the Light... not the light made by man but the Light that made man,"* I wrote in my spiritual novel *The Epic of Arya – In search of the Sacred Light*.

Enough of religious fundamentalism, ignorance, superstition, and delusions: ***we need to (re)discover the real God, not the "God" created by man*** (and religions) but the God who created man. That is what spirituality strives to do. That is the noble mission of all the spiritual guides and masters who have trodden this earth throughout the ages: Krishna, Buddha,

Zarathustra, Mithras, Christ, Hermes, Orpheus, Pythagoras, Plato...

Ex Deo Nascimur: we are born from the Divine. That is what spirituality teaches us. That is the God I am talking about when I resolve to "believe." Belief, viewed in this deep, spiritual sense, is none other than the link with the divine source whence we sprang. *Answering the question "does God exist?" therefore depends on how we view and define God.* The real God is not the personal, anthropomorphic god who is separate from his own creation, but the Divine that dwells first and foremost in man's inner depths.

God is not separate from Nature. God *is* Nature. Does Nature exist? Yes; therefore God exists. Pantheism has been lambasted by religious people for its "sacrilege" that lies in equating God with Nature and fusing the divine with the human. Yet this is the only scientific as well as spiritual truth and fact: *God is in All and All is in God. Ex Deo Nascimur.*

And yet a certain degree of scepticism is often-times needed, or rather, needed at all times. Doubt is important, useful, and even necessary for the mind, for it enables us to avoid falling into the throes and pitfalls of superstition, and pushes us to use reason, that God-given gift which separates man from the animals. Doubt allows us to be lucid and to make decisions based on our critical reason, instead of our fallible senses. However, pushed to its extreme, doubt leads to denial, and denial leads to nihilism and despair. Therefore, along with a certain degree of doubt, we should develop a higher kind of faith, not blind but enlightened faith which opens new horizons for our souls thirsting for infinity and unity with the Source whence they sprang.

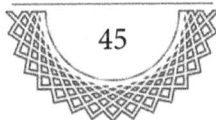

"I shall believe": this in no way means that I should fall on my knees and pray before a distant and unknown "god" in heaven, as religious people do. Rather, it simply means that I shall believe what is in me — my very soul — and what is right there before my eyes, the mystery of life (call it Cosmos, Nature or "God," it is the same mystery); I shall believe in the secret behind the higher intelligence, Consciousness or Force that governs the cosmos of order and harmony sometimes draped in chaos and mayhem.

Despite all the progress of the past century in terms of physics, technology, medicine, etc... science has yet to provide answers to the great mysteries of Life. If religion has given the wrong answers, science has given *no* (definitive) answers, only prompting more questions. The Big Bang theory is one among many examples of the limits of science; it has yet to be proven. Thus the mystery of life, of creation, of "God," remains complete, as there are infinite possibilities and no certainties.

Man is a thinking being; but, more importantly, he is also a spiritual being with a deep need and natural propensity for faith. The religious sentiment and spiritual longing and aspiration are inborn in us. This longing that takes hold of our souls from cradle to grave is our link with the divine; animals do not have that divine instinct and consciousness that characterises human beings. That is because men are, as Teilhard de Chardin wrote, *"spiritual beings having a human experience."*

Faith is the essence of happiness, for it keeps us connected with the Source, with the Whole; it is a spark of the divine Light of Truth which we all seek — consciously or unconsciously — throughout our lives. It is our link with the eternal, infinite energy that pervades the universe. Whether one calls that energy "God," "Spirit," or "Force," does not matter; what matters

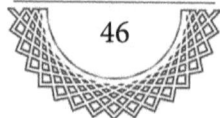

is that this energy — called ether or the "quantum energy" by scientists and physicists, or *Fohat* by spiritual people — this energy has been proven to exist and is made up of invisible vibrations, waves. Even scientists admit that there is something beyond matter, "anti-matter," a subtle invisible energy that permeates all and everything. Quantum physics supports this concept and underscores the importance of consciousness as having a direct influence on the material world, the observer, or subject, influencing the observed, or object.

So why should we have faith in God or the universe, or simply life? *Without faith, nothing great could be accomplished.* Without faith, we would become alienated, disconnected atoms floating aimlessly in space, wretched creatures who lead aimless, empty lives. Enlightened faith is our link with the mysteries of life; it opens new horizons for our inner infinity to explore the unfathomable depths of the universe.

If "beauty is in the eye of the beholder," faith is in the heart of the believer. Enlightened faith gives us hope and connects us with the *Geist*, the Spirit and higher purpose of life. It is in the heart that the soul of God dwells, for there is no faith without love, and love is the breath of God.

What is wrong with the world today? The world we live in drowns in darkness, the darkness of ignorance and unbelief, of idolatry and nihilism, these twin enemies. In the West, there is a crisis of meaning and purpose caused by the "death of God" and the nihilism and agnosticism that ensued; in the East, there is a crisis of reason and freedom caused by the scourge of religious fundamentalism, which is the death of the spirit.

"God is dead," announced Nietzsche to the dispirited, disillusioned world. God was killed by both cold reason (atheist materialism) and blind faith (religious fundamentalism). The

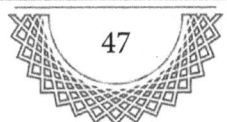

inborn religious sentiment in man, his need to believe in the soul and in God, to be connected with the All, this sentiment has been stifled by excessive scepticism and agnosticism (and hence nihilism) in the West and by fundamentalism and fanaticism in the East.

What is the impact of such unbelief — or false belief — on the world? Ignorance, darkness, spiritual and moral decay. Why is it so? Both extremes — religious fundamentalism as well as atheist materialism — deny life, the former by putting God above life, in an unreachable "heaven," the latter by denying the deeper dimension and higher meaning of life, the soul, which is a spark of the Soul of the World. When God is either idolised or shunned, life loses its meaning and purpose, as man forsakes his divine destiny and either kneels or denies.

Thus, both fundamentalism blind faith — and materialism — cold reason — kill our soul by denying the deeper dimension and higher meaning of life. The perennial conflict between science and religion, between reason and faith, this conflict itself has "killed God," for God is whole, life is whole, and man is only complete when his faith and his reason are united — this is what I have called "enlightened faith" — when body and soul coexist in perfect harmony. As I wrote in *The Epic of Arya*, *"reason without faith is cold and empty, and faith without reason is blind and dark."*

Materialism and fundamentalism are two extremes that are the daughters of ignorance, for they both sever man from the whole, the Source which is One. Matter and spirit are two facets of the same energy manifesting and operating at different levels. When we separate them, we are also severing our soul from its very essence, its Source and its end.

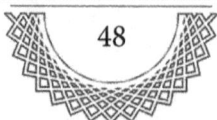

Agnosticism and materialism forbid us from perceiving and experiencing higher, subtler realms, for, through them, we deny the existence of a higher, spiritual dimension, we shut ourselves out of the world, we separate ourselves from the whole; thus we deny our higher selves, our souls. Fundamentalism, on the other hand, separates God from his own creation, from man, as man is reduced to being a servant of a tyrant-god "above the clouds," with no possibility of redemption in this world. Thus, both materialism and fundamentalism lead to life denial and hence to spiritual decay. They both lead to denying man his higher purpose and his higher destiny: to become divine, in God's image.

Thus, "enlightened faith," faith in the soul, in the divine that dwells in us, that kind of faith is the subtle, divine energy that connects us with the whole, with the soul of life. The truth is that God is neither above life nor dead; God is in us, God dwells in us, we are in God, we are God manifested. The soul is something in the body and at the same time outside of it; the other dimension suffuses and manifests itself in this dimension. *The two worlds — material and spiritual — mix and merge in the bosom of life.*

Belief in the soul is the source of life affirmation, elevation and self-fulfilment, which is the essence of happiness. There is a higher dimension in life and within man, whether we call it "soul" or "God" or "God within." It is the Soul of the World that creates and perpetuates life. Ours is a universe filled with mysteries, everything is possible, all possibilities remain open. We should therefore keep an open mind, we should be free spirits ever seeking deeper, farther and higher. To be is to believe, and to believe is to be. And to believe is to love, for there is no faith without love, love of the highest: God. Love

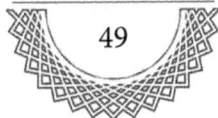

is the soul of life and the breath of God; it is an inexhaustible source of joy, our link with the bliss of eternity.

My formula for finding inner peace and happiness, for receiving the blessing of faith, is to develop a higher love through the perception of higher worlds: God dwells in me; in other words:

"Atman Is Brahman."

This is the eternal truth of the Vedas, whereby *Atman*, the breath of life, the soul, is one with *Brahman*, the Spirit, God. Existence is Absolute Unity and we are part of this whole; enlightened faith is the higher consciousness that connects us with the Source, the All.

By believing in another, higher dimension, which nonetheless is immanent in nature, we open ourselves to the world around us, we become spirit and matter united in harmony and purpose. Thus we participate in creation. We develop our will to live in a higher sense, we find meaning in, and give meaning to, our lives. Motivation and creativity then characterise our transformed life. We become complete human beings.

Only when we are complete are we truly happy. And we are only complete when our faith is reconciled with our reason, when our faith is governed by reason and our reason is imbued with faith, when God is in our heart and when we are in the heart of God, as the great Gibran wrote.

What is the impact of such an attitude on us and on the world? When we embrace faith in life, in this world of daily miracles and wonders, we unite with life's soul and purpose, we live in peace and harmony with ourselves and with our

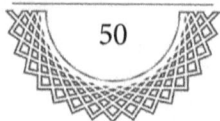

fellow humans as well as all other living creatures. Our world can therefore function as a harmonious whole where we complement each other and thrive and blossom together to glorify life and live it abundantly.

THIRD RESOLUTION

I Shall Have Faith In Life
And In Myself

"The snow falls, each flake in its appropriate place."
– Zen saying

WHY IS IT important to have faith in life, faith in the meaning and purpose of life, and most importantly, faith in oneself? If we are to trust life, it must have a meaning and hence we must have a purpose to fulfil in the grand scheme of the universe, each of us in his or her own way and according to his or her own nature, abilities and aspirations. Otherwise, without meaning, all would be vain and nothing would have any value, not even life itself; and the world would become a huge graveyard of souls and an endless sea of heartache and despair.

From time immemorial, man has asked himself this ultimate existential question: "does life have a meaning?" And, if so, what is it? If not, why do we bother to exist at all, given that everything is doomed to death and oblivion? Throughout the ages, man has sought to find a meaning in life — or, when he failed to do so, to *give* life a meaning — and he has striven to achieve the meaning which he has assigned to life. For life is only worth living when we bestow a meaning upon it, our own meaning, according to our own path, the deepest law of our nature, our life purpose and vocation, our *Dharma*.

Man is the evaluator: he creates symbols and gods, bestows value and meaning upon things and people, as well as upon life itself. Everything that man sees, hears, feels, becomes imbued

with meaning. For man cannot live without a purpose; and where he does not find it, he invents it. His *Horror Vacui* ("fear of the void") forbids him from living a meaningless life. Atheist philosophers even claim that this fear of the void is the very reason why man invented "God," not the other way around. The world should make sense for us to bear to live in it. Hence each one of us has a dream that keeps him alive and makes him get up every morning full of hope and aspiration, despite life's many trials and tribulations.

However, when tragedy occurs, when there is death, loss, illness, war, violence, injustice, etc... life seems unfair, absurd and meaningless. More often than not, life seems to be a haphazard sequence of random events, blind matter in motion. Life's absurdity — or rather, what we *perceive* as life's absurdity (since we do not behold the bigger picture, being ourselves part of the picture) — leads us to question why bad things happen to good people, and good things happen to bad people. In these dark moments, when nothing seems to make sense, we doubt the existence of God and doubt that life has any meaning.

Despite that, most of us still act according to our conscience, guided by that inner voice which tells the good from the bad and right from wrong. And yet life does not seem to make sense anymore, in this world of greed, selfishness, and deceit. Thus we fall into disillusionment; we become nihilists and surrender to despair, cursing our dark fate, and even God himself. We lose faith in God and in life, and, most importantly, we lose faith in ourselves.

Is there a God? Is there a higher intelligence that governs our universe? Does life have a meaning and a purpose? And, if so, why does evil exist? Those who firmly affirm that life has a meaning, the religious types, tend to assign an outside meaning

to life and hence they believe in an "afterlife" which is nothing other than an escape from the suffering, woes and ills of the real world. These religious people fall into fatalism: they accept everything that happens to them in this life with resignation, without any resistance, waiting for a better life in the beyond, after the "liberation" of death. Theirs is not a will to live but a will to die, as death is viewed as the ultimate liberation from an unworthy life of suffering. *"We will get salvation in the other life, the next life,"* the religious people thus console themselves, *"now we should endure this life, for all is written."*

The other type, the other extreme, the sceptic atheists, the materialists, affirm on their part that life has no meaning and that the universe is just "blind matter in motion." Thus, when bad things happen, they tend to fall into nihilism, which preaches that "all is vain," that life is absurd, and that we are doomed to oblivion: *"from dust we are made and to dust we return,"* these nihilists affirm. Consequently, they either become nihilistic, even suicidal, or indulge in hedonism, living life "abundantly." Life to them becomes a mere pursuit of pleasure and comfort devoid of any higher meaning. However, despite "living life abundantly" (as *they* see it), these atheists remain empty inside, hollow shells with souls thirsting for a meaning, for a higher consciousness and self-realisation.

Both the religious and the atheists end up denying life, the former by inventing a "beyond" as an escape from this life and a "God" that is above life, forever unreachable and unknown, the latter by denying the higher meaning and dimension of life, and refusing to believe in the spiritual dimension of the material world or the "God within." The rest of us — whether realists or idealists — are caught and lost between these two extreme visions of life and, unwilling to kneel or to deny, we

struggle through life trying to extract a meaning from its many riddles.

When tragic events occur and we are faced with what we perceive as life's absurdity and meaninglessness (due to the flawed interpretations and erratic attitudes of both the religious and atheist types), we again ask ourselves the inevitable questions: "does life have a meaning? Is there a God?" Yet even in the darkest moments, our will to live pushes us to refuse to give up on our built-in faith; we feel that beneath and behind all the suffering and injustice that characterise our world, still there is a reason why these things happen. We console ourselves by repeating the mantra that God's will "acts in mysterious ways," although we honestly cannot understand why a "God" would allow so much evil and suffering in this world.

Tragedy causes us to lose faith in life, and yet something, some hidden hope and longing, remains deep within our souls. Our faith is shaken but never totally stifled. That is because *the religious feeling is inborn in man.* Man has an intuitive affinity with the Divine, a natural propensity to trust and revere life. Even the atheist is merely in a state of denial, denial of his spiritual essence. The truth is that our souls all have a longing for unity with the Source, the *Geist,* and *our lives are a search for wholeness through self-realisation.*

By intuition, against all odds and despite the many woes that we endure throughout our life, we feel the presence of a higher Force governing this universe of great beauty, order and harmony. Whether we call this force "God" or Life or whatever name we choose, this force is also present in us. **We are the meaning of life.** *We* are God. We are agents of this superhuman force, co-creators, sons and daughters of Nature.

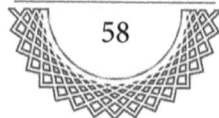

Thus the meaning of Life becomes intertwined with the meaning of *our* life. Those of us who adopt this attitude start believing that everything happens for a reason, that we are alive for a purpose and that *life is just providing us — whether through challenges, disappointments, or even tragedies — with opportunities for spiritual growth and creative evolution.* Indeed, the aim of life is not "happiness" but endless creation and elevation which take place beyond good and evil, beyond joy and sorrow, even beyond life and death.

In contrast to the fatalists who believe that "all is written" as well as the nihilists who affirm that "all is vain," the "magical realists" — a new breed of idealists who believe in perfection in the here and now — believe that we are alive for a reason, that life has a meaning, but that this meaning is not to be sought outside but rather inside our very souls. We are here for a reason, and life is nothing but a series of opportunities — and tragedies are also opportunities for spiritual growth — which we either seize or ignore.

Therefore, when we realise that we alone are accountable for our own acts, *we stop playing the victims of "fate" and start taking responsibility for our own thoughts and actions.* No one else and nothing else is held accountable for our successes or failures, neither "God" nor any other force but us. That heroic, Stoic attitude towards life is what Nietzsche called the "great liberation."

The Good, the True, the Beautiful, Love, Virtue, Justice... these are all manifestations of the divine Light, what Plato called "Universals," objective absolute values. But Light cannot exist without darkness; the Light needs darkness to be. Indeed, we live in a world of opposites, of duality; there are various facets to Being. There is diversity in unity, and unity in diversity.

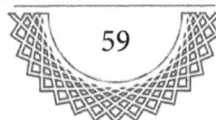

Therefore, God is both light and darkness, life and death, spirit taking form in matter, beyond good and evil. This duality, these dialectics which characterise the human world enable us to become conscious and complete human beings. Through the world of matter, the world of forms, our souls become self-conscious and self-fulfilled. Creation only takes place through dialectics, when Being and Becoming mix and merge.

Life does have a meaning, but that meaning is not outside life and outside man; that meaning is life itself in its totality, in its higher forms and manifestations. *The meaning of life is creative evolution and eternal self-overcoming.* This higher meaning is not to be sought outside life and outside ourselves, but here on earth and within the depths of our souls. Our life bears the meaning we give it. Each one of us has his own meaning and his own purpose, his own path and his own destiny, according to his own potential and abilities. And yet like the notes of a symphony, we all participate in that cosmic orchestra that is eternal creation.

Life is God, God is Life: this is my pantheistic vision of the universe which, unlike the religious vision, does not separate God from his own creation. There is a "God," but God is not outside or above Life. *The creator and the creation are one.* God is the conscious universe, a living organism; *God lives in us and through us,* He breathes and thinks through us. Therefore, we must live life in its totality, we must live all the seasons and cycles of existence. Thus we participate in the dance of the universe and sing its celestial melody as sons and daughters of Life.

We should think of ourselves as co-creators connected to the higher Force that moves the worlds. Only thus do we participate in and contribute to life's evolution. We are agents of change

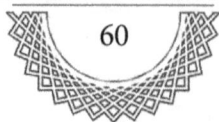

and of evolution, but we can also be agents of destruction and decay if we do not serve life and ennoble and elevate it. The power is within us; how we use it depends on the path that we have chosen for ourselves.

The law of life is evolution; its aim is elevation; its end is eternal creation. Evolution happens in cycles and spirals of birth and rebirth; death is but a prelude for rebirth. We are agents of the divine creative force which pervades and moves the universe. *Our purpose on this earth is to fully live our individuality and to awaken to our higher self and fulfil our divine destiny,* which is none other than becoming gods ourselves, "perfect as our Father in heaven is perfect." Our purpose is to fully live our freedom as independent entities whilst being conscious parts of the Whole, microcosms that reflect the timeless, infinite Macrocosm.

In fact, it is the Spirit of the Earth — *Gaïa* — which is becoming self-conscious and self-fulfilled through us, its parts. Therefore, we should live life in its totality, for *"all is for the best in the best of possible worlds,"* as Leibniz wrote. The world makes perfect sense, and we only realise that when we tune into its universal frequency and forget our individual worries and concerns. We achieve that "transcendence in immanence" by becoming the higher, better version of ourselves, by developing all the human virtues which are also divine virtues.

"How wonderful! How wonderful! All things are perfect, exactly as they are," said the divine Buddha: The world makes perfect sense, for there is order, purpose and harmony in life. Therefore, despite evil, chaos, violence, injustice, illness, sorrow, loss, and all the woes that plague existence down under, still, we should maintain our faith in life, because everything happens for a reason in the grand scheme of the universe and serves to

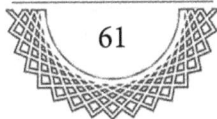

awaken and elevate us. Indeed, our purpose in life is to become conscious of our inherent divinity and to evolve into gods. Therefore, we should relish the blessings of life and endure its tragedies, for creation and elevation take place beyond good and evil.

"God gave me nothing I wanted, He gave me everything I needed" said the great Hindu master Swami Vivekananda, who introduced Hinduism to the West. Whatever happens, we should have faith in Life, for Life gives us what we need, not what we want; for what is best for us, for our spiritual evolution, is not necessarily what we desire for ourselves but what life's higher destiny has in store for us.

We should therefore strive to give meaning to our life, for our life is a blank page upon which we write our own destiny. What we reap is what we've sown throughout our life. We write our own story on the pages of history, on the Book of Life, and that story itself determines our fate and our future, whether in this life or — for those of us who believe in reincarnation — in the next. The past determines the present, the present determines the future. Thus evolution is endless creation.

Nature revolves in endless cycles of birth and rebirth; and, as we are the sons of nature, our eternal souls, which are the life force that moves us, take on different forms throughout their incarnations. This is what the Hindus and Buddhists call the Law of Karma. We are ruled by this law, as karma is the fruit of our own free will, thoughts and actions; we determine our own karma throughout the ages.

Therefore, there is no accountability; no one but us is responsible for our present situation. There is a higher wisdom behind events which we ourselves have created; these events are symbols of our inner life. The significant people whom we meet

and the meaningful events that we live are all reflections and symbols of our inner evolution, our soul's evolution across the ages.

And so we create our own destiny through our free will and through what C.G. Jung called our "personal myth." Our present life is the consequence of our karma, our deeds in a past life and in this life. We created our own circumstances throughout the incarnations and we continue to create our present and our future. We keep recreating ourselves forever anew.

That is why we should trust life, for we have made events happen, we create the future every minute of every day, through our thoughts and our deeds. It is all a question of will. *Karma is "divine" justice that we ourselves create:* we have the free will to decide whether we evolve or go backwards, whether we do good deeds or evil ones, whether we elevate life or degrade it. We have a divine gift: the blessing of free will. No one and nothing else is accountable for what befalls us. It is neither "God's will" nor random and arbitrary chance. **Our will creates our destiny.**

Life is but a mirror of our souls; it reflects what it sees. The seeds we sow are the fruits we reap. Life will give us back what we give it. By serving and elevating life, it serves and elevates us; by denying it, it denies us. Therefore, we should have faith in ourselves before we can have faith in life. *"You cannot believe in God until you believe in yourself,"* said Swami Vivekananda. We have created our own circumstances, our own life, its sorrows and joys, its successes and failures. It is up to us to change it for the better or for the worse.

"The Lord acts in mysterious ways," the saying goes (yet the "Lord" is none other than Karma. *We* are God). Only by looking at the bigger picture can we understand the wisdom behind every event — good or bad — that befalls us. There

are lessons to be learned in everything that happens to us. In fact, something that may seem bad has meaning, serves to turn us into better persons, serves to awaken us. In the world of opposites, the light needs its shadow to be. *"Every cloud has a silver lining"*; it is all a question of perspective and attitude: whether we look at the cloud or at the silver lining, whether we act or submit.

My formula for finding inner peace and happiness:

"To man belongs the will, and to God belongs the way."

This quote, taken from my inspirational novel, *The Epic of Arya – In Search of the Sacred Light*, entreats us to strive to realise our full potential so that life will meet us halfway and open all horizons to our aspiring souls.

Do your best, always, for what you give life, life gives you back. Your will, your thoughts, your deeds are realities, they determine your destiny; you reap what you sow throughout your life and across the ages. Everything that happens is the fruit of your own will. There is a higher intelligence that governs the universe and connects people and events. Everything happens for a reason, and that reason lives in you, it is your soul's growth and self-fulfilment. Everything has its cause in you and the solution always lies in you.

Outer circumstances serve as the setting, the arena of life, but you yourself are the actor, the creator of your own life, the captain of your own ship: destiny. Therefore, relish and embrace the good with gratitude, endure and learn from the

bad with fortitude. Accept and live the seasons of life and know that behind every challenge and every misery, there is an opportunity for growth, wisdom and creativity. There is meaning and purpose behind every event. Tragedies are more often than not opportunities for spiritual awakening, growth and self-realisation.

Consequently, we should behold the broader, brighter picture, even in the gloomiest times. Evolution takes place beyond good and evil, which means that even the darkest events bear a meaning and a purpose. We only understand that in hindsight, when we are able to behold the greater picture and see meaning in what seemed unjust and absurd earlier, when we were caught in the midst of the tragedy.

Therefore, weep over the departed, accept and live your sorrow, face your problems, but always know that through these problems and unfortunate happenings, and even tragedies, something greater will arise; rest assured that life has something better in store for your soul's evolution on the pathway to completeness and self-fulfilment.

If we have the will, God will show us the way. Have faith in life, but first and foremost in yourself, for you are a co-creator and a Son of Life, a Son of God at the crossroads of the human and the divine. Take control of your life, do not surrender or submit to "fate," for fate is something that *we* ourselves create, as the just law of karma dictates. Life gives you what you give it; or, as the popular saying goes, *"what goes around comes around."* Like attracts like; have faith in life, do your duty, follow and live your dream, and it shall come true.

Suffering breeds awareness and creativity. Life wants us to create; it will give us what we need to grow spiritually and to awaken to a higher consciousness, whereby the divine breath

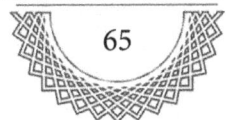

fills our souls and liberates our minds. The aim of life is not happiness but creative evolution, and we are the happiest when we create and overcome ourselves, when we create beyond ourselves and serve eternity. But as I said above, evolution takes place beyond good and evil.

Therefore, when something bad happens, when tragedy — the loss of a loved one, illness, a painful breakup — occurs, tell yourself: *"this is my karma; what did I do to cause this? I am a co-creator, I have caused this to happen, partially or totally. I am not a victim of circumstance; whatever happens to me, I have willed it or caused it or at least contributed to it with my will, my thoughts, my acts, consciously or unconsciously, in a past life or in this life; that is the law of attraction which rules the universe. Therefore, I can change it or transform it into something useful and creative."* And if you cannot change it, then it was meant to be, it is your higher destiny, and you should accept your fate and move on. Or, as the Dalai Lama, with his joyful wisdom, says: *"If there is a solution, why worry? If there is no solution, why worry?"* In fact, tragedies are sometimes great opportunities for spiritual growth.

If I am a victim of an injustice, my mission is to fight to eliminate that injustice. If I have suffered a great loss, my mission is to immortalise the spirit of the departed loved one and to uphold his or her values. Whether or not we have — directly or indirectly, consciously or unconsciously — caused what happens to us, the important thing is how we deal with the situation. If we have faith in ourselves, we'll have faith in life. If we have faith in life, we'll have faith in ourselves.

Trust life, for everything that happens, happens in order to awaken us and to make us evolve into better human beings, into spiritual and divine beings. It is only in hindsight that

we understand that everything that happened *should have happened* for our life to make sense, for *there are lessons to be learned even in what seems utterly absurd or unfair.*

By adopting such a healthy attitude at all times, whatever the circumstances, I find and give meaning to life according to my own soul and my own will. Do your duty and follow your dream, evolve following the path you have chosen, and go with the flow, for you have caused that flow with your own thoughts and deeds. And even if events that befall you are out of your control, view them as opportunities for change and growth. When things seem to go wrong, strive to change them by doing the right, honourable thing, by following your conscience and your good judgment. But cling not to the fruits of your action, for "*que sera, sera,*" whatever will be, will be; in the end the good, the just, and the true always prevail.

Worry not about the results or the fruits of your actions, for you are the seed and life is the harvest, thus you shall reap what you have sown, whether in this life or the next. With such an attitude, anxiety, worries, and fear disappear, life suddenly makes sense, and we enjoy its many blessings and endure its tribulations with patience and fortitude. *Thus we learn to turn every challenge into opportunity and every tragedy into wisdom.*

FOURTH RESOLUTION

I Shall Not Judge

"Judge not, lest ye be judged."
– Matthew 7:1

W E ARE ALWAYS judging; judging persons, things, ideas, creeds, events, judging life itself. Man is the evaluator; he has even made God in his image, turning him from loving Father into a ruthless judge. Judging is a natural reflex: we observe, we see, we hear, hence we think and judge; I am, therefore I judge. We spend our lives judging. Good or bad, right or wrong, beautiful or ugly, lofty or base, etc... that is how we view things; our minds are full of value judgments, all day long, all year long, and for the rest of our lives.

Why do we judge? There are many reasons for that but the answer boils down to this: we judge because we are always comparing the outside world, the others, whether they be persons, ideas, or identities, with ourselves, with our own identities and beliefs. We want life and the others to be so and so, thus we reject what *we* perceive as "bad," "wrong," or "ugly" etc... yet *who* is evaluating? Our mind. And our mind is conditioned by who we *think* we are, our identity, whereas the truth is that our soul is our only reality, for it is eternal and infinite, it alone survives after death, while the body returns to the earth.

The particular judges life and the others, the particular that I am judges the particular that is out there, unaware that this

particular is an integral part of the Whole, and that I myself am an integral part of the Whole.

When we judge, we separate and divide that which is essentially one: Life, the universe, God. For there is a fundamental unity between all living creatures, one energy that encompasses and pervades the entire cosmos. The One manifests and expresses itself in the many, unity blossoms in diversity. When we judge, we are separating ourselves from the Whole. It is the ego that judges. And the ego cannot live without an identity. Its identity is its fetters, and yet it still clings to its chains, for it derives meaning from these very chains. *Ideas and identities become prisons when they become ends in themselves.*

How do we judge? We judge according to who we are, or rather who we *think* we are. Who are we? We define ourselves according to our identities: race, nation, class, culture, religion, political affiliation, etc... Based on these identities which define us, we screen others through the lens of our own identities, our own prejudices. Most of these prejudices are a reaction to our interaction with other cultures, religions, nations, races... but some of them are *a priori* prejudices based on an idea — whether true or false — that we have about some groups, mainly based on generalised, oftentimes arbitrary stereotyping: "Americans are vulgar," "women are shallow," "the English are cold," "the French are arrogant," etc... in reality, stereotypes tend to be the exception, not the rule.

Every man is an island. We are ruled by our egos which need to separate and divide in order to exist. We refuse to see the whole picture and instead we see through not our infinite, eternal souls, but rather through the eyes of our egos which are full of prejudices; that is how we judge life and the others. That

is why the outside world remains an inhospitable place for most of us. As the French say, *"c'est chacun pour soi"* — "each fends for himself" — in a cruel, unfriendly and atomistic world.

With the notable exception of thinkers and spiritual masters who are free spirits, humble seekers of truth, the rest of us tend to think that we have the monopoly of Truth, Morality, Beauty, etc... the truth is that despite our much-vaunted "tolerance," deep inside, most of us are convinced that only we know what is wrong and what is right, what is good and what is bad, what is beautiful and what is ugly, what is lofty and what is base according to our own standards: "that man is stupid, that woman is vulgar, that child is ugly, etc..." We would like to make the world in our own image. If we had our way, the world would be this or that way. That is fine, but what if — and that is often the case — what if the others disagreed or had *their* way? One man's dream is another man's nightmare; one man's heaven is another man's hell; ***one man's god is another man's devil.***

If we look at world history, we see that, throughout the ages, there has been a conflict, a clash of ideas, creeds, ideologies, religions, visions of the world, civilisations... a conflict about "Truth," "God," the Good, Justice, Liberty, etc... Each and every creed and religion openly or surreptitiously claims supremacy over the others and tries to impose itself on the others. The result is strife, tension, war, violence, division, crusades, "Jihad," etc...

"Judge not, lest ye be judged," said Jesus Christ, as he beseeched us to look at the log that is in our own eye instead of seeing the speck that is in our brother's eye. Judging has only begotten wars and hatred between people and among people of the same race and nation. Judging is based on division and separation, and all it breeds is hatred, division and separation because it is based on the ego which thrives on evaluating,

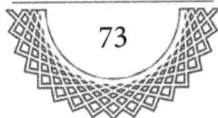

labelling, separating and dividing according to identities, beliefs and standards; that is the way the ego survives and asserts its disconnected, atomistic, alienated identity. The ego breeds conflict and survives and thrives through conflict.

The soul, on the other hand, is one with the energy, the Spirit that imbues and moves the entire universe. It needs to unite with the world, with the Whole, with life, with God, and consequently with the others who are part of this Whole. Altruism is a natural result of such a spiritual attitude whereby some benevolent persons help and serve those in need. Indeed, spiritual persons have what one might describe as a "thrust towards unity," as they see the Universal and the Eternal behind the particular and the transient. The soul breeds peace and harmony and thrives through peace and harmony.

However, if we simply affirm that we should never judge, without giving this resolution a moral dimension, we run the risk of falling into moral relativism, where the worst deviances and perversions become allowed, justified and even desired in the name of "freedom" and the liberal slogan of "live and let live." Total lack of judgment is thus as nefarious as judgment based on identity and beliefs. The former leads to moral decay and decadence, the latter to bigotry and fanaticism.

So what is the solution? Is there a right attitude that prevents us from judging, whilst preserving the universal values that mankind has upheld since time immemorial? The solution lies in upholding morality whilst preserving diversity and safeguarding freedom. How is that done? By judging people (or rather perceiving them) not based on their identities or beliefs but solely on their *acts*, their conduct. That is the only way we can measure a person's morals: by his actions. Actions speak louder than words: *"you will judge them by their fruits,"* Christ said.

Man has a conscience. It is a divine intuition, the voice of God within his soul that guides his conduct and makes him distinguish what is good and right from what is bad and wrong. The supreme virtues: Truth, Justice, Beauty, Goodness, etc... are Universals, or so they are supposed to be. Yet that is hardly ever the case on the ground, in peoples' and nations' attitudes towards each other. Almost everyone agrees on these Universals, these universal ethics. Those who do not agree are not human, do not deserve to be called human. They are outside the human race. Every normal human being agrees on these universals, every religion and political creed claims to uphold these universal values. The problem lies in *defining* them. That is where humans disagree: defining what is true, what is right, what is good, etc...

Therefore, in order not to fall into either moral relativism or conflict, we must define these universals *away* from our prejudices towards identities, creeds, and dogmas. In other words, these universals must remain universal, absolute, and not become particular and relative to fit our own particular identities. No compromises or exceptions should be made on these universals, otherwise they cease to be so and sometimes even turn into their very opposites. For example, justice and freedom should not be reserved for or limited to a certain group but to all of mankind; goodness is goodness at all times and in all places; love is for all living creatures, not just our own kind; nobility is nobility of soul, regardless of birth, etc...

The spirit that dwells in every man should commune with other men as spiritual beings and not dwell on the fleeting, shallow forms, which are but the vehicle for the soul. So long as we do not perceive others away from these identities and creeds, judging will breed tension, hatred, violence, incomprehension,

for each group and each individual will want to impose their own point of view or vision of the world on the others, claiming that they alone have the monopoly of the "Good, the True, and the Beautiful."

So let us endeavour to pinpoint these universal values that are mankind's collective dream of perfection and harmony. These universals, according to the major religions and philosophies of life, are the following (the list is very long but may be summarised by these main values and virtues): Truth, Goodness, Beauty, Justice, Love, Nobility, Honesty, Humility, Purity, Courage, and Generosity. Those who do not share these universals are outside the human paradigm and against our human conscience which forms the basis and the spirit of all religions and all value systems.

Therefore, we should judge people and things not according to *a priori* prejudices and stereotypes but according to their conduct in conformity with these universals. Instead of looking at life and at the others from our own narrow perspective and prejudices, we should view our fellow humans through the moral lens.

My formula for peace and happiness:

I shall judge man not according to his identity but according to his conduct.

We should look beyond identities (race, class, nationality, religion, culture, or political affiliation) and judge a person according to his conduct which reflects his morals, his conscience and the true nature of his soul. In simple, layman's

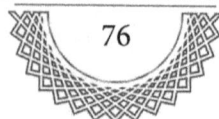

terms, this attitude is summarised by the popular saying *"do not judge a book by its cover."* Similarly, **do not judge a man by his identity but by his soul, which transpires in his deeds.**

We should judge life as it is: perfect order, a Whole, divine Unity, and consequently act according to the voice of our conscience which is dictated by these universals that are present in the collective psyche of mankind. Our conscience is part of the collective unconscious of mankind, the universals which are the same for everyone on this planet. Thus there should be impartiality regarding identities; morality alone should be the judge and the jury, and morality manifests itself through our deeds.

The problem lies in the fact that most men agree on these universals, but they disagree on how to achieve them. The truth is that the means should not be different from the ends. The means never justify the end; they either ennoble or debase it. Therefore, follow Immanuel Kant's categorical imperative while achieving these universals. The categorical imperative, which is the central philosophical concept of Kant's moral philosophy, reads as follows: *"Act only according to that maxim whereby you can, at the same time, will that it should become a universal law."*

We should strive to have an ideal conduct, we should be in line with these universals in our daily conduct, decisions, actions and relationships with others. *"Be a light unto yourself,"* said Krishnamurti, echoing the Buddha's main exhortation. I would like to extend that sentence to encompass mankind as a whole: *"be a light unto yourself and unto the world."*

This positive attitude and conduct leads to peace and harmony between men, as we act according to our conscience which reflects God's Spirit. And in this peace and harmony lies the very essence of happiness.

FIFTH RESOLUTION

I Shall Accept Change

"Everything is in flux."
– Heraclitus

OURS IS A world of becoming, of evanescent realities; change is a part of life, indeed, the very essence of life. The human realm is ruled and characterised by impermanence. Life revolves in cycles of birth, death and rebirth. Nothing remains the same on earth. *"Everything is in flux. No one bathes in the same river twice,"* said the wise Heraclitus.

Although we aspire after eternity and perpetual bliss, what the Buddhists call *Nirvana,* the truth is that we actually live in an ever changing world. Evolution is the law of nature and the nature of life. In fact, although it is often painful, change is necessary; becoming is creative evolution. Without change, there would be atrophy and decay. Of course, the ultimate change is death, which is also a kind of rebirth in a different form. Even death is a parenthesis, a pathway towards a new life, a transformation of the soul, and not an end in itself.

Why is change more often than not painful? Why do we almost always suffer when change occurs? We suffer because we resist change, we refuse the natural and inexorable flow of time, ageing, and all kinds of changes in our personal lives and the world that surrounds us. We humans need security, stability and certainty in order to overcome — or at least to hide — our fear of the unknown and ultimately, our fear of the greatest

change: death. This resistance to change makes things painful, it breeds sorrow and anxiety.

Why do we resist change? First of all, there is fear of the unknown; fear of growing old, fear of losing friends or loved ones, and, ultimately, fear of our own inexorable demise. Then comes the need for stability and security, and the longing for eternity, the quest for the peace and bliss of eternity. We only want the "ups" of life, refusing and dreading its "downs"; we do not accept life in its totality, in its cycles and seasons, which involve birth, blossoming, decay, and death... and rebirth. We all want to live in a perpetual spring, and yet deep inside we know that it is impossible... and so we suffer.

There is no "eternal spring"... and, come to think of it, maybe that is for the best: indeed, how boring life would be without its seasons, and the unique charm of each season! Life has its ups and downs, ours is a world of change and contrasts, opposites, which are ultimately fused in a higher unity, in the oneness of Being. Yet *even the darkest night is pregnant with the light of day*. Sometimes what seems like a bad event is actually a blessing in disguise, an opportunity for growth, yet we only realise that when we look at the bigger picture, and that always happens in hindsight, long after the unfortunate or painful event. We look at our past, our path, and we understand why things happened the way they did, why they *should* have happened *that* way and not any other way.

However, we seldom look at the bigger picture, we are too engrossed in the details of life, failing to behold its grand scheme; and so we reject and resist change, either living in denial or falling into total depression or apathy when (painful) inevitable and irreversible change does occur in our lives: having to move to another city or country, changing jobs (or,

worse, getting fired), parting with friends, losing loved ones, etc... as painful as these events may seem, they are necessary, for that is the law of life, which revolves in cycles.

What is the result of such resistance to change? Resistance to change and to the natural flow of time leads to suffering, anxiety, and even life denial, since by doing so we deny life's very law and nature, which is transience, eternal becoming and transformation. Consequently, we become alienated, always resisting what is inevitable — and oftentimes necessary — simply what *is*. Denying or refusing change is tantamount to denying life itself. This wrong, unnatural and unhealthy attitude causes stress, anxiety, and all kinds of suffering and frustration.

What, then, should be our attitude towards change? A loved one dies... we lose our job... we move to another city, another country... our children leave us to live on their own, etc... how do we deal with these unsettling changes in our lives? Of course, in extreme cases like death or illness, pain is unavoidable, at least at the beginning. After all, we are only human and all of us are bound to face illness or death one day. However, after the initial shock and the necessary, natural and even healthy grieving period (denial being more lethal than depression, for it only postpones it and worsens it), how to deal with our new life? How to avoid having a negative, even nihilistic attitude towards life after our great loss or other upheavals that turn our lives upside down? How to keep our faith in our life and our destiny in spite of the pain, fear and anxiety caused by change?

We should develop and adopt an objective "witness attitude" towards life, whereby our inner core, our soul — or *"unencumbered self"* — remains detached from and unmoved by outside events. *The silent depths of the sea remain untouched by the restless waves of its surface.*

We are infinite, eternal souls, not particular, perishable egos. When we draw a clear distinction between soul and ego, and thus distinguish between the essential, the eternal on the one hand and the fleeting and illusory on the other hand, we break free from the shackles of the external world and its impermanence, which brings with it many woes, trials and tribulations. Awaking to our true nature is our great liberation from the fetters of the material, evanescent world of forms. *"I am That I am"*; in other words, "I am conscious that I am conscious": this is how the spiritual awakening burgeons and blossoms, when we become aware of a higher consciousness beyond and above our finite ego. This is the witness attitude.

The healthy attitude that we should adopt is to perceive life as a stage in a play, and we as spectators watch events unfold without judging or assessing, but simply observing the flow of life unfold before us. This objectivity is also known as equanimity, which means not allowing events, be they good or bad, to affect our mood or state of mind; not being the victim of change, of life's many ups and downs, but rather being life's objective witness, developing a higher consciousness and awareness, awaking to a higher, broader perspective and a wise, peaceful and positive attitude towards life.

We still enjoy life's many pleasures and "ups," yet we don't allow ourselves to become identified with our possessions, our status, our social roles. That detachment shields us from the pain associated with earthly attachments.

True, lasting happiness is not external, not dependent on external factors or events. True happiness is the result of inner peace of mind, and a healthy and positive attitude towards life. Therefore, we should accept change — however painful it may be — as something inevitable, the very nature and law of life.

Change is necessary in life and for life to continue growing and thriving; *change is necessary for creative evolution.*

Without progress, without evolution, life would stagnate, decay and die. Nothing endures under the sun, save the immortal soul which reflects the Soul of the World. Yet even the individual soul must at one point leave the body — which is only a vehicle, a cloak that it borrows to realise its full potential and embrace the creative thrust of existence — and take on a new form in a new birth or another world or dimension.

The soul alone is eternal, indestructible, unchanging, and yet it lives and takes form in cycles and spirals of evolution and involution, of blossoming and decay, of death and rebirth. This is the essence of creative evolution, which is none other than the deeper meaning and higher purpose of life.

My formula for peace and happiness:

"We are all passing waves, and what remains is eternity. Therefore, cling not to the waves, but embrace the sea."

(The Epic of Arya – In Search of the Sacred Light).

Enjoy the good times with gratitude, and endure the bad times with patience and fortitude, but do not get attached to the transient, fleeting things, for they are all doomed to fade in the mist of oblivion; and what remains is Eternity. *We cannot control events, but we can control our reaction to these events and our inner state of mind.*

This, of course, does not mean that we do not life live fully and abundantly; it only means that we do not get attached to material things (or our social status or image, what C.G. Jung

called the *persona*, as opposed to the *anima* or soul) so as not to define ourselves by those externals and so that we do not suffer when we lose them: beauty, money, status, power, possessions, career... "*You only lose what you cling to,*" said the wise Buddha. Life is eternal becoming, constant change. Resisting change only breeds suffering and frustration. *The end of attachment means the end of suffering.*

Yet attachment to people, to fellow human beings, is a totally different matter and is unavoidable; after all, this is what makes us human. Love is attachment, attachment inexorably leads to loss, and loss of a loved one always leads to suffering. But, as Queen Elizabeth II said during Princess Diana's funeral, "*grief is the price we pay for love,*" quoting the beautiful, wise words of Dr. Colin Murray Parkes, a psychiatrist at St Christopher's Hospice.

The full quote deserves to be included in this book about happiness, since love is the essence of happiness; here it is: "*the pain of grief is just as much part of life as the joy of love: it is perhaps the price we pay for love, the cost of commitment. To ignore this fact, or to pretend that it is not so, is to put on emotional blinkers which leave us unprepared for the losses that will inevitably occur in our own lives and unprepared to help others cope with losses in theirs.*"

Death is the ultimate change. Loss of a loved one always leads to suffering. Pain is unavoidable in the realm of mortals, it is joy's dark twin, and both are daughters of life. Therefore, accept and endure your pain, but later, after the grieving period, try to move on with life which goes on, inexorably, eternally, by embracing the sea instead of clinging to each evanescent wave. Granted that these "waves" might have been persons who were very dear to us, who were our soul-mates and companions,

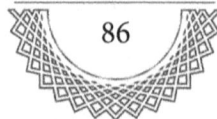

still, we should bless the beautiful moments that we spent together and treasure these memories in our hearts forever. But remember that the ocean shall claim us all one day, and we shall meet again in a new dimension of being, in the depths of eternity.

Tragedies and other bad events and painful changes shall befall you... and grieve you should and shall; but ultimately, life goes on... therefore, learn to accept its cycles of death and rebirth, of ends and new beginnings — for *ends are always new beginnings.*

As for other painful — but less tragic — changes, we should learn to perceive and use them as opportunities for spiritual awakening, growth and progress, as growing pains or labour pains, if you will. More often than not, change is creative, it is necessary — and sometimes even a prerequisite — for creation and creativity.

"When God closes a door, somewhere he opens a window": as I said above, every end is a new beginning. Therefore, when change knocks on your door, tell yourself: *"I shall accept change, for it serves my destiny and my self-fulfilment. What I desire is not necessarily what is good for me; and conversely, what befalls me is always what is best for me, for my spiritual evolution."* Always remember Heraclitus' wise words: *"everything is in flux."*

When change is painful, as it often is, tell yourself: *"this too shall pass,"* as the spiritual teacher, Eckhart Tolle, wrote in his important book, *A New Earth.* Offer no resistance. Do the right thing, do what feels right, what is necessary, but do not resist what is ultimately unavoidable. Surrender to the law of life, whilst at the same time doing your best to achieve your aims. Yet do not cling to the fruits of your labour, for *"everything is for the best in the best of possible worlds,"* as Leibniz, that most

optimistic of philosophers, said. It may not seem this way when the painful change or tragedy occurs, and yet everything is in your best interest, not your narrow immediate and transient ''happiness" but your soul's elevation and self-realisation.

Tell yourself that change is always an opportunity for evolution, for awaking to a higher level of consciousness. The fact that change often brings pain should not make us forget that it is necessary. Did not the great Nietzsche entreat us: *"become who you are?"* We can only become who we are if we evolve, and so change is healthy and necessary. Accept it and you will find inner peace, harmony, and happiness.

As we apply this resolution, we learn to endure and even enjoy the various seasons of life and we evolve into better, higher and wiser beings at peace with ourselves and with the world.

SIXTH RESOLUTION

I Shall Bond With Others

"A friend is a second self."
– Aristotle

WHY IS IT important to bond with others, fellow human beings, to make friends and have meaningful relationships? As Aristotle affirmed, man is a "social animal"; he also said that only a god or a beast could live totally alone, completely isolated from mankind (*"to live alone one must be a god or a beast"*). For good or for bad, man is destined to live in society; even the most introverted type needs to have some form of human contact in order to live and to function as a human being. It is impossible to be happy without relationships (lover, family, friends, acquaintances, etc...): *"happiness is only real when shared,"* wrote the author of that beautiful book (and later movie), *Into the Wild.*

Solitude might bring happiness to thinkers, writers, and artists who need it in order to draw inspiration from it, to create and to realise their full potential; however, total, constant solitude is both unhealthy and impossible, lest one lose his humanity. Living in total isolation would not be living at all. It would be living on the margin of life, outside life, not participating in the whirlwind of becoming, the dance of the Cosmos.

We need the others to live a full, happy life, just as cells in our body can only function as parts of the whole, fulfilling their own respective functions whilst cooperating with one another

(a cell that secedes from other cells becomes cancerous, and so it is in the human realm). Love is the blessing of life and its essence. Living without love, without relationships, would turn us into dead men walking, lonely creatures in search of a soul.

In our modern societies characterised by competition, materialism, selfishness, what prevails is tension, hostility, and incomprehension. Citizens tend to be isolated atoms struggling for survival, competing for power, authority, and status. True love, true friendship based on compassion and honesty is hard to find in our materialistic, utilitarian world driven by greed and the lust for power and money. The result is dysfunctional relationships between men and women, between friends, colleagues... which leads to control or manipulation by some of others. Thus, love turns into hate, friendship into adversity, harmony into conflict.

Why is it hard for us to establish meaningful relationships based on trust and friendship? It is because in this material world obsessed with sex, power, money, fame, the ego reigns supreme; and the ego separates and divides, it is ruled not by love — which unites — but by desire and its dark twin, fear. Thus it seeks to control the others so that it can survive and thrive as a separate entity.

According to the ego's twisted logic, others are perceived as rivals or foes. It is "me" against the others, a Hobbesian nightmare or "war of all against all," even if this "war" often and mainly remains surreptitious, undeclared and takes form in competition and adversity.

Honour, loyalty, honesty, are rare assets and nearly extinct values nowadays. Chivalry is all but dead and with it its morality, which is true humanity. Relationships in our modern age are based on fear of the others. This fear leads to tension,

conflict, alienation, and to an atomistic society of lonely individuals whose relationships are governed by utility and opportunistic manipulation, which leads to strife, domination and oppression.

A healthy, ideal society is a community of individuals who share common values, a common dream, and hence a common destiny. This harmonious, peaceful society is rare to find nowadays, except in remote villages where tradition is still revered. Yet even in cosmopolitan, multicultural societies, one can still find something in common with others, some solidarity with like-minded people.

There is always a common ground between us and our fellow men: common interests, common hobbies, common beliefs, common values, etc... therefore, it should not be difficult to establish friendships based on these common things. *No man should be an island.*

My formula for healthy, meaningful, deep relationships:

Look for the light in everything and everyone, and you shall find it.

Find out what you share with others — it could be as shallow as a common hobby or as meaningful as a common cause — and let this bond be the basis of either a pleasant relationship or a communion between kindred souls. We do not choose our family, but we do choose our friends, who are our extended family. The French have a saying which summarises the basis and secret of enduring friendships: *"qui se ressemble s'assemble"* ("like attracts like").

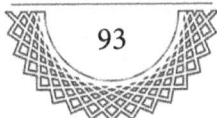

There is always a way to find common ground with people. Look for that common ground, those common values, *seek the Light in everyone you meet, and you shall discover your unknown brothers in the strangest places.* Give others a chance, and you will make surprising and meaningful friendships. Just keep an open mind — and, more importantly, an open heart — and you will spread and find the light everywhere.

The light that your soul emanates will be reflected in the light that dwells in the soul of other human beings. *Thus it will not be mere "like attracts like" but "light attracts light."* Bonding with others thus becomes possible and a new and beautiful friendship could then blossom.

What is the result of such a positive predisposition and attitude towards the others? Compassion, sympathy, harmony, sound, deep spiritual relationships; a spiritual brotherhood which is above and beyond social divisions and national borders, but, more significantly, above and beyond the borders that we draw within our hearts and minds. Thus a shared spiritual experience can emerge and bloom, making the world a better place to be in and life a pleasant and meaningful experience to be shared among kindred souls.

SEVENTH RESOLUTION

I Shall Have A Positive Attitude

"How wonderful! How wonderful!
All things are perfect, exactly as they are."
– Buddha

W HY IS IT important to have a positive attitude and positive thinking? *"You are what you think,"* goes the famous axiom, echoing the timeless voice of wisdom of the eternal Vedas. The truth that few men know and accept is that we become what we think, that our thoughts become realities, that we shape our own world. We are always having thoughts, ideas keep popping into our minds every second of the day; and so we are always creating our reality, we are eternally becoming, eternally transforming ourselves and recreating ourselves ever anew.

Therefore, in spite of life's many challenges and difficulties, it is important to always maintain a positive attitude. Otherwise, if we choose to look at the dark side of things, at the half-empty cup, and never see the silver lining but focus on the dark cloud of gloom, then, instead of becoming the captains of our destiny and the creators of our own happiness, we become the victims of our despondency, of our negativity. We reap what we sow throughout our life (and, for those who believe in reincarnation, throughout our lives), thus we decide our own destiny. *Fate is our own creation.*

However, most men and women remain impervious to the fact that their negative thoughts poison their lives and

perpetuate their misery — and lamenting instead of acting only makes things worse —, thus they remain negative most of the time, most of their lives. It is indeed rare to find a truly positive person in our modern world characterised by competition, greed, selfishness, tension, and struggle for power. We are just too negative and pessimistic.

Consequently, by remaining negative, we lose faith in life and in ourselves, and, when faced with a challenge or a problem, we surrender to despair and we curse the world we live in and sometimes doubt the existence of God, asking ourselves: *"how could a perfect God create an imperfect world?"* Fatalism thus becomes a natural reflex. The result is a feeling of "doom and gloom" which often leads to outright atheism, life denial, and — in extreme cases — suicide.

The law of attraction, "like attracts like," turns our negative vibes and thoughts into actual events which in turn have a negative, destructive influence on us, on our inner state of mind; and so the vicious circle perpetuates itself eternally.

How to break this vicious circle? How to take control of our life instead of surrendering to frustration and despair? First, a higher awareness — and a sense of responsibility — is necessary: realising that no one else but us is accountable for what befalls us. This knowledge must be accompanied by an acceptance of the nature of the world we live in. Indeed, the human realm is a world of contrasts, opposites, a world ruled by dialectics: there is no "up" without "down," no "good" without "bad," no "positive" without "negative." In fact, the negative makes us appreciate the positive, even makes the positive possible. Moreover, the positive emerges out of the negative, even as light emerges from the midst of darkness. It is a necessity, it is the way things move in the material world.

If we learn to look at life from this perspective, we will learn to endure and overcome the negative in our lives. The Greeks considered that suffering leads to knowledge, that knowledge is impossible without a certain degree of suffering, and that creation is always born of suffering. It is from the darkest depths that dawn is conceived. One should therefore always look for the positive in everything and everyone.

In my book, *The Epic of Arya – In Search of the Sacred Light*, I wrote *"all joy hides a secret pain, every beauty bears an inner scar, and the pleasure of today is but the tears of yesterday and the regrets of tomorrow."* Yet pain will also turn to joy, and tears to laughter, in the circle of life. We have to learn to accept the nature of things, if we want to live a happy, meaningful and creative life. There is wisdom behind this duality: these dialectics, (to use Hegel's term) are what turns the wheel of becoming, the wheel of creative evolution. Becoming is the law of life, and this happens in cycles and seasons, this happens through contrasts: joy and sorrow, good and bad, right and wrong, light and darkness, elevation and decay. That is the nature of life which revolves in cycles.

In order to survive in this world of becoming — which is full of suffering and hardships — and to fulfil our highest potential and therefore be the persons we were born to be, we should first accept life as it is while at the same time adopting a positive attitude in order to "ride the wave" and to go with the flow, before we finally embrace the ocean of infinity whence we came. Self-realisation is the final aim, and this can only be done through awareness of the nature, law and purpose of life. *Awareness brings acceptance, and acceptance brings peace.* Positivity thus becomes our best ally and tool for evolution and progress.

As we accept the nature of things and the flow of life, which is creative evolution that takes place beyond good and evil, we cleanse our inner temple, our soul, of the poisons that corrupt it, poisons that are linked to external things — things which oftentimes turn into obsessions — like sex, power, money, fame... These poisons that destroy our souls are none other than fear, hatred, greed, envy, lust... we should undertake a *tabula rasa* of all these emotional poisons before they consume our souls and turn us into hollow shells and desolate hearts.

From the void that follows this cleansing process, a feeling of spiritual plenitude and contentment arises: this is none other than our purified soul blossoming anew after it has rid itself of all that is alien to it: the dust and darkness of material illusions and delusions.

However, problems will still arise and negativity will always plague us, for we live in an imperfect world. So how to keep a positive attitude at all times, despite life's many annoyances, frustrations, problems, and tragedies? There must be something higher than these problems and frustrations and even the many dramas that haunt us from cradle to grave. What is it?

My formula for peace and happiness:

"Sub specie aeternitatis."

This Latin phrase means *"from the aspect of eternity."* It was used by Spinoza and later by Schopenhauer. What does it imply? Annoying little things lose their importance and become less unsettling and frustrating when they are viewed *"from the aspect of eternity."* In the grand scheme of the infinite universe, only the essential remains; nothing else matters. Everything passes; what remains is eternity.

One should always behold the bigger picture, focus on one's greater destiny, and think and act accordingly. Extract the positive from the negative; *turn suffering into wisdom, and every challenge into an opportunity.* Always look for the silver lining in every dark cloud; it is there, if you just look closely with the eyes of your soul. It is all a question of perspective: whether the glass is half-full or half empty, whether things are viewed from the aspect of our tiny, perishable egos, or from the aspect of eternity, our greater destiny.

You should change your outlook on life and learn to turn an unfavourable or even tragic situation into an opportunity for awareness, awakening, and creativity. After all, all creativity derives from suffering; every birth is made in the greatest pain. Always look for the higher meaning and purpose of your life and forego the little annoying things — and people — that stand in your way. They have no importance *sub specie aeternitatis.*

Since *"like attracts like,"* we should constantly watch our thoughts and monitor our emotions and try to maintain a positive attitude at all times, or at least most of the time. We should see the meaning behind negative events and, instead of surrendering to despair, ask ourselves: *"what lesson is there for me to learn in order to evolve spiritually?"* When something bad happens, we should endure it by considering it a passing dark cloud in an otherwise spotless sky. Out of suffering emerges consciousness, and out of consciousness knowledge and creativity.

Sub specie aeternitatis: Eternity is the only reality; nothing else matters. Only by living for and serving eternity, and thus leaving a trace in history, do we truly live and glorify life. And yet, in everyday life, when dealing with material, temporal and transient reality, merely repeating this magical formula

is sometimes not enough, especially when we are trying to make ends meet and survive in this world of struggle and competition; indeed, there are very real problems that plague us during our life on this earth, and some of them are simply too hard to overcome. So how do we deal with our daily problems and our ever-present pain?

First, by viewing things not as problems but as opportunities and milestones on our spiritual evolution; second, by integrating them into our higher scheme, our greater destiny. *"Something better will come along; life has something better in store for me"*: that is what our attitude should be when problems seem too overwhelming. Concentrating on the greater scheme of things and our place in that greater scheme makes our problems and our pain seem less important, as we view them as opportunities and milestones on our higher path towards enlightenment and self-fulfilment.

I live, therefore I suffer. I love, therefore I suffer. Suffering is our lot as humans. Schopenhauer used to address humans as *"my fellow sufferers." No one can escape suffering. Yet it is how we deal with our suffering that makes the whole difference between leading happy, meaningful lives or miserable lives filled with anxiety and despair.* The difference between a happy man and a miserable man is not linked to power, money or status, but rather it depends on how one views life, how one deals with his suffering, how one transforms his suffering into something creative and beneficial to himself and to the world at large.

Happiness is an inner state of mind, an attitude towards life, a question of perspective and perception; it is not to be confused with joy — which is ephemeral — , desire and pleasure, which are linked to external factors and are more often than not a

mere gratification of the senses. As the spiritual teacher Deepak Chopra said, we should not allow external rewards like power, status, money, possessions, to replace inner growth. It should be the other way around: the external world is the arena, but *we* are the actors, the subjects, not mere objects of consumerism. We should not confuse the means with the end. *The end is essentially and always the imperishable soul and its evolution towards divinity.*

However, unlike what is falsely widespread, real non-attachment is not renunciation or abstention; it is not the extinction of the ego, but rather the freedom from externals. *Externals do influence us but they should not define us.* They should be means towards higher ends, but never ends in themselves. We are not our social status, our possessions or our bank account; we are eternal, boundless souls that thrive beyond borders towards a higher consciousness, towards self-fulfilment and self-overcoming.

I live, therefore I suffer. Would I rather live and suffer, than not live at all? It is true that we do suffer a great deal in life, but we also experience joy and enjoy the beauty and harmony of this earth and the pleasures of life, as well as the blessing of love. There is always the other side of the coin. That is the side we should always behold and uphold, come rain or storm, for, above the dark clouds, the sun shines eternally. That positive attitude is our stairway to a happy, higher, meaningful life.

Contentment is the secret of happiness. Whenever you feel dissatisfied and negative, practice contentment by "counting your blessings." Be grateful for all that God has given you — there is always something, there *must* always be something that you appreciate about your life! — and how fortunate you are; and know that *everything that happens — good or bad —*

serves your inner evolution. By comparing yourself to your less fortunate fellow humans, you start appreciating the blessings that life has imparted upon you, and thus you develop gratitude and contentment. And, of course, you feel compassion, you feel compelled to help these less fortunate beings.

The result of such a positive, healthy attitude towards life is that we do not let bad events or negative people affect us, we maintain equanimity and *remain immune to negative influences by focusing on the higher and deeper meaning of our lives.* Thus we steer the wheel of our life in the right direction. The wind will always blow, yet we set our sails to navigate our own way, on high seas, until we reach our destination and fulfil our destiny. Contentment thus becomes our permanent state of mind and well-being.

EIGHTH RESOLUTION

I Shall Not Dread Solitude

"All man's miseries derive from not being able to sit quietly in a room alone."

– Blaise Pascal

WITH THE NOTABLE exception of thinkers, artists, spiritual masters and mystics, humans in general tend to dread solitude and seek out company. While solitude is sometimes necessary — and even desirable — for finding inner peace and inspiration, and for meditation and contemplation, it is more often than not synonymous with loneliness, which is a different thing. Solitude needn't — and shouldn't — be loneliness... in fact, we need some quality "alone time" with ourselves, every now and then, for introspection and connection with our deeper self, our soul.

Solitude could be a great opportunity for spiritual growth and intellectual and artistic creativity; it is even a necessity. Loneliness, on the other hand, stems from a feeling of emptiness, of inner void and fear of the unknown which makes us dependent on situations and people (and even ideals and beliefs) as an escape from that inner void. Addictions and obsessions are an attempt to escape that inner void which haunts our souls when we are alone.

What is the problem with being alone? Most of us fear solitude, we fear being left alone facing our mirror, the mirror of our soul, the mystery of mysteries... thus we seek out company in order to avoid facing life's perennial existential questions

and unsolved riddles: *"Who am I? Why am I here? What is my destiny?"* Most people spend their entire lives outwardly, evading the essential and thus escaping their real purpose on this planet. They flee solitude as one flees the plague, losing themselves in idle entertainment or petty worries just so they would not experience the dreaded face-off with themselves.

Why do we dread solitude? Solitude forces us to face our Self, our inner core. And most of us are unable or unwilling to do that; unable because we consider the material world as the only real world and ignore the deeper spiritual dimension, the inner infinity, our immortal, unchanging self which lies at the source of all that exists; and unwilling because we cling to the world of the senses, to our basic instincts and craving for power, sex, and money, and ignore our inner self, our soul, which is the only thing that is eternal and real in us. All possessions will one day be lost, but our souls are our inner infinity. All we take with us to the grave, to the other life, is the one thing we truly *are*, that which is immaterial, immortal: our soul. Naked we are born and naked we die.

However, most of us remain empty inside and thus we try to fill this abysmal void in our souls by losing ourselves in others (friends, family, politicians, gurus...) or in external things (symbols, creeds, ideologies, religions...), in order to escape our Self. This creates unhealthy addictions and tense or unequal relationships, instead of healthy self-contentment and self-fulfilment and relations based on a communion of kindred souls.

Our materialistic world based on competition, greed and tension between atomistic isolated individuals imposes solitude on us, the fact which makes it unavoidable, at least some of the time. The question is: how to bear it? The solution does not lie in seeking company; that is only an escape. The real cure is to

stop dreading solitude and manage to live with ourselves and to face our souls. *"Know thyself,"* goes the famous Pythagorean axiom. Only when we know ourselves can we establish healthy and meaningful relationships. *Peace starts within.* Sound, solid friendships are based on complete, independent human beings interacting with one another.

What would the ideal attitude be? To be able to face ourselves and be alone without being fearful, bored or despondent. The ego, which, turned outwardly, constantly lives in fear and thus needs to separate and divide everything in order to feel secure and in control, should surrender to the inner self which, filled with love, is united with life's very soul and purpose. *Only when the ego subsides will the soul expand.* Only then will we become whole, balanced, healthy human beings. As stated above, a certain dose of solitude is often necessary for a person to develop spiritually and intellectually and discover his purpose. The real you lies in your soul; in *The Epic of Arya – In Search of the Sacred Light,* I wrote: *"the divine lies in the depths of your undiscovered self."* Know thyself, and thou shalt know God.

"No man is an island": none of us is alone at the spiritual level. There is a sacred, imperishable, infinite and invisible presence: the Self, which is a spark of the divine consciousness that pervades the universe. We are a medium for God. God is becoming aware of Himself through us. We only need to discover that divine, eternal being and presence that dwells in us and imbues us with the breath of life.

The self is God. God is the Self. An anonymous Christian heretic expressed this truth in these beautiful words: *"if you do not make yourself equal to God, you cannot perceive God."*

We are God. That might and will sound blasphemous to religious people and ludicrous to atheists, and yet this is the

spiritual reality. We are quantum energy, spirit pervades all and gives life and form to matter. Matter is just a lower level of vibrations; condensed spirit, as it were. We are microcosms. The universe is in us.

My formula for finding inner peace and happiness:

Be Your Own Best Friend.

Enjoy your own company and delve into your own mystery, your inner infinity; after all, no one else knows and understands you better than yourself! Take time to meditate and to discover your inner world of thoughts and feelings. I call the time I spend on my own, thinking and meditating, my "magical time," for it is the only time I can get in touch with my soul in the stillness of being, delve into my inner world and mystery, and thus truly know myself. Through this knowledge, I can have a better understanding of life's meaning and thus live it fully and abundantly.

"One can be instructed in society, one is inspired only in solitude," said the great Goethe. Turn your alone time into quality time. *Life is an inner journey of self-discovery.* Ultimately we are in search of our soul, our undiscovered self. Man's nature is triune: the body belongs to the material realm, the soul belongs to the human realm, the spirit belongs to the divine or spiritual realm. The synthetic, complete man — as opposed to what Nietzsche called ''fragmentary men'' — is he who has achieved perfect unity and harmony between these three worlds, and lives in all three dimensions at once and in harmony.

God exists, thinks and creates through us. Therefore, we are never really alone. We are co-creators. We are the drop in the

divine ocean, we should bathe in that ocean whence we came and whither we go. The atheists think that by venerating God, we are worshipping ourselves second-hand. This is quite true, but in a much deeper sense, for God dwells in us, the divine breath — or *Atman* — dwells in our souls. We are the rays of the divine Sun, we are the drops of the divine ocean. In fact, we are the drop and we are the ocean.

The religious person says *"God is great,"* putting God above himself and above life, and hence denying life. The atheist says *"there is no God,"* dismissing the higher dimension of life, and thus also denying life. The spiritual person, who believes that the creator and His creation are one, says *"I am God,"* thus affirming and glorifying life. The truth is that there is no separation between man and God. Man is a god in the making, God is the future of man. We should thus develop divine consciousness, we should discover that we are God, that we are divine in essence and that the universe is an intelligent living organism. Everything is intertwined in the complex web of creation.

It is only when we are alone that we can draw inspiration from the depths of the cosmic mysteries and reach awakening. Therefore, we should not dread solitude, for in its silence God breathes and life blossoms and sings its celestial symphony to our exalted soul. *Solitude is a great opportunity for inner growth, self-discovery and self-realisation.* In its divine silence we transcend our finite ego and discover our immortal, universal self.

What is the impact of such a spiritual attitude towards life? When we discover the "other," deeper dimension of being, we reach wholeness, inner peace and harmony and can then set out to realise our full potential in life and engage in meaningful

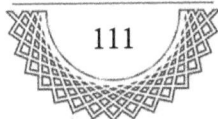

encounters with fellow human beings. And then we are able to build and establish healthy relationships and solid friendships. When we discover our inner infinity, we are at peace with ourselves and the world, which will thus be a better place to live in.

NINTH RESOLUTION

I Shall Be Independent

"Sing and dance together and be joyous,
but let each one of you be alone,
even as the strings of a lute are alone,
though they quiver with the same music."

– Kahlil Gibran

IN OUR AGE of interdependence, in this "global village" that the earth has now become, where we rely on so many things and factors to function properly in society, how can we be truly independent, autonomous? Few of us can, few of us are... indeed, we rely on technology, we are dependent on the market and its fluctuations, our jobs, our government and its policies that have a direct impact on our lives, etc... To be independent in the modern age is therefore a difficult, semi-impossible task.

We are attached to so many people — family, friends, politicians, religious leaders — and so many things, we depend on so many "externals": money, power, possessions, position, career... we define ourselves by our status and beliefs; we are conditioned by education, advertising, and most of us (regretfully) totally rely on the opinion of others for evaluating our own worth. Our sense of identity is mainly shaped and determined by what others think of us. We are the captives of society. The cage may be made of gold and beautifully adorned, yet it is still a cage that we live in, as we are totally dependent on our environment (and its deterioration directly affects us).

Why are we the prisoners of material things? The ego thrives on having, while the self (or soul) blossoms in being. Thus, more often than not, the ego achieves external fulfilment and success but at the heavy price of internal void, death of soul and poverty of spirit.

What is the consequence of such dependency on people, ideas and beliefs? There is the danger of domination, manipulation or exploitation by others, which leads to pain and disappointment. As for our addictions to externals like power, status, money, sex, etc... they lead to perpetual frustration since the satiety of the desire gives rise to another desire in an eternally vicious circle.

What, then, needs to be done in order to stop being dependent on the outside world? We should achieve autonomy, the autonomy of the soul, regardless of other people and external influences. It is true that there is a fundamental unity of all things and that the world is interconnected, yet a certain degree of independence is both healthy and necessary. *Unity should not become uniformity.* We must maintain and develop our individuality, for unity manifests itself in diversity.

Our ego, which is just the tip of the iceberg of our deeper being called the unconscious, is influenced by the outer world, and yet *our soul is a world unto itself;* it is our inner, eternal, indestructible self which no one and nothing can hurt or alter. Our soul is unchanging, indestructible, imperturbable, immortal. Our ego is moved by the turbulent winds of life, but our soul remains unchanging even as the depth of the ocean is unmoved by the waves of the surface.

However, dismissing the ego altogether is both impossible and unhealthy, for it plays an essential role as the medium between the soul and the outside world; it is the vehicle of our

soul. It must function in society and fulfil its various duties if we are to become fulfilled and sociable citizens who live life fully and abundantly. What should happen is a harmony between the ego, which is dependent on externals, and the self or soul, which is our deeper essence. The soul should determine the ego's attitude and behaviour, not vice versa as the materialists maintain and as is — alas! — the case with the greatest majority of people.

This process of integration of the ego and the self, of the outer and the inner, is what C.G. Jung called "individuation." Through it we become complete human beings.

Our soul must remain an impregnable fortress of peace and wisdom at all times, impervious to other people and events, upheavals, tragedies... *The secret of happiness is a healthy and rich inner life.* The outer world is a world of becoming based on struggle, tension, chaos, and mayhem, whereas the inner world is a world of being, a world of peace, order and harmony.

A balance between the inner and outer worlds should be reached for us to realise our full inner potential and outer achievements. We should remain spiritually detached from the shackles of the external world whilst fulfilling our social duties, objectives and ambitions. Involution — the soul's inner unfolding — should beget evolution — the soul's manifestation in the world. *The involution of the soul manifests itself in the evolution of the personality.*

My formula for peace and happiness:

Cultivate Your Inner Garden.

Cultivate the garden of your soul. Nourish your soul (through music, art, poetry, spirituality, etc...) as you nourish your body,

its temple. Play your social role and strive for success and fulfilment, but do not forget who you truly are, your true self, your inner core.

Attachment is human, detachment is divine. Awaken the "silent witness," the consciousness that is aware of being conscious. But I do insist that non-attachment should not mean or lead to renunciation and the rejection of the outer world, for we depend on it and fulfil ourselves through it (as said above, involution leads to evolution); rather we should always remain grounded in our self whilst functioning normally in society. Thus we develop inner strength, strength of character and healthy and meaningful lives in accordance with the nature of our soul, our true nature.

TENTH RESOLUTION

I Shall Do Good Deeds

"Je sais et je sens que faire du bien est le plus vrai bonheur que le cœur humain puisse goûter."[2]
– Jean-Jacques Rousseau

W HY IS IT important, for our emotional and spiritual well-being (and the well-being of mankind), to do good deeds and spread joy around us? All religions extol the "good," and philosophy sets the pursuit of "the good, the true, and the beautiful" as its highest goal. When we do good deeds, we are tuned to a higher energy, our soul becomes joyful, purified, and uplifted; it soars in the higher spheres of being.

"To be doing good deeds is man's most glorious task" said Sophocles. The Rig Veda on its part affirms: *"the person who is always involved in good deeds experiences incessant divine happiness."* By doing good deeds, we feel inner joy and satisfaction, we feel as though this is our real nature, our highest potential; we feel close to God, we become divine. However, the sad fact is that the good is widely promised and praised but seldom lived and bestowed.

In our world filled with evil, hatred, violence, dishonesty, deceit, envy... there is little empathy and compassion, as only selfishness and greed seem to govern the relationship between

---

[2] *"I know and I feel that doing good is the truest happiness that the human heart can taste."*

men. This is the sorry state of the world we live in. Even in peaceful times of prosperity, good deeds are rare; they are the exception and seldom the rule. *Homo homini lupus*: "man is a wolf to man." This Roman proverb by Plautus perfectly illustrates the dark world that we live in. *"The Light once touched the face of darkness, but darkness chose to look away,"* I wrote in my book *The Epic of Arya – In Search of the Sacred Light.* Man has yet to be blessed by the Light of Christ, Son of God, highest and purest manifestation of the Good.

We spend our lives striving to satisfy our desires and to realise our ambitions, not paying heed to what is really essential, what really matters, and that is: alleviating the plight and suffering of our less fortunate fellow humans, people in need of help in the form of food, clothing, money, or just moral support. Our over-inflated egos have neither the time nor the willingness to help others. We are obsessed with success and thus forgo *what life is really about: love, empathy, peace and harmony.*

Why is that? Why is the world filled with so much evil? Why is it hard to find a genuinely disinterested good deed? In our dark age, the ego is king; and the ego is concerned — even obsessed — with itself and nothing else. We are isolated atoms living in the small cocoon of our vain egos. Selfishness rules supreme. We have all but lost our humanity. Lust has overcome love: lust for power, money, sex, possessions, status... we are but the shadows of what we can and should be. I, me, mine: that is how we view the world, through the lens of our narrow egos.

The problem is that, most of us, instead of viewing our ego as a mere instrument, a vehicle for our soul's self-realisation, our soul's higher destiny, instead of that, our ego with its many desires and cravings becomes an end in itself; thus we lose sight

of our true vocation in life, which is the union with the divine, and that union is always realised through the gift and blessing of love, love for all living creatures under the sun.

The ego separates and divides, it wants to grab, control and possess, for it lives in fear and insecurity; it is entangled in the frantic dance of becoming, whereas the soul thrives in the stillness of Being and strives to bestow the infinite love that dwells in it. The ego thinks of its own narrow desires, success, pleasures, power, etc... whereas the soul, being connected with the Soul of the World, the Supreme Good, wants to beam its light unto the world, it wants to give back to life the many blessings that life has bestowed upon it. And *the greatest blessing is the blessing of Love.*

Egoism versus altruism: that is the difference between the narrow, perishable ego and the infinite, immortal soul. The problem is that most of us are attached to our *persona*, our social image, and pay little heed to our soul, our inner essence or self. The result is a society of alienated individuals locked in constant competition, tension, hatred, and violence. In such a world, there is no room for empathy or spiritual evolution, which is done through enlightenment, compassion that transpire in good deeds. Every man becomes an island, disconnected with the very essence of life.

In contrast to the present world, what would the ideal world be like? If man had the divine qualities, if man were truly *"in God's image."* Divinity is best embodied by and manifested in the Good: love, compassion, selflessness, altruism, are divine qualities. Having what the French call *"le sens des autres,"* compassion for the others, brings us closer to God.

My formula for finding peace and happiness:

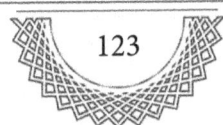

The Good Is God.

By doing the good, we are united with God: Good and God are the same. By doing the good, I become divine, which is my true, deepest essence. Haven't you noticed that divine feeling of satisfaction and contentment that fills your heart when you do the good? It could be through charity: giving money to the poor and helping vulnerable groups (the elderly, orphans, etc...), or through moral support: being there for your friends and family, helping out someone in need, maybe a total stranger, or any selfless act intended to uplift life and ease the suffering of others.

The separation between me and the world, me and the others, is illusory. The material world gives us the impression that it is made up of separate entities, yet in truth matter is just condensed energy, our bodies are our souls' lower levels of vibration. Ultimately the same energy pervades the universe. Our egos seem like separate entities, yet in truth, we are all interconnected, we all form the Spirit of the Earth, Gaïa. Therefore, feeling empathy, sympathy, compassion for others, helping them, doing good deeds, is our soul's true nature and our true calling.

The world is one. We are one. That is the reason why we feel joy and inner peace when we do good deeds: this is our true, divine nature. When we do good deeds, we are in sync with the very essence of existence. We are programmed, inclined by our very souls to do good, to help those in need. The unity of existence manifests itself in love for others.

Think positive, do good deeds, expand your soul. Thus you uplift life and serve its meaning, thus you reach out to touch the face of God and sing his celestial melody. The good is God; by doing the good, you become divine, a god in the making.

Be there for a friend, a relative, a colleague. Help a homeless old lady, adopt an orphan or at least bring a smile to his face by buying him toys. Be there for your loved ones. Help a total stranger in need. Spread love and joy around you, and your heart will be filled with the bliss of divinity.

Do one good, disinterested deed a day, from the heart and not because you have to or are expecting anything from it. That would be enough: one good deed a day... if that is too hard, start with one good deed a week, then make it a daily bestowing. But, most importantly, the good deed should be totally selfless and disinterested; you should expect nothing out of it: no reward in the "next life," no "good karma," only the satisfaction of having fulfilled your duty as a human being, having fulfilled your humanity.

The atheist who helps out the poor, expecting no reward "in heaven," is a more ethical human being than the religious person who gives out of interest, expecting to reap the reward of his good deeds in the afterlife.

However, it is important to note that helping others and being a little selfless does not mean not loving oneself and not fulfilling one's own desires or ambitions. The Good is not self-denial, which is neither healthy nor natural. It only means we leave a little room in our souls for the others, those less fortunate, those who need a helping hand. It means we count our blessings and try to share these blessings with our fellow humans.

A life of service brings joy to the world but also to our own heart. The great Indian Poet Rabindranath Tagore expressed this truth in these beautiful words: *"I slept and dreamt that life was joy. I awoke and saw that life was service. I acted and behold, service was joy."*

The result of such a lofty and noble attitude and such a selfless behaviour would be a world of peace and harmony, a world without war, tension, violence, greed, a little piece of heaven on this earth. That may seem like a utopia to sceptics, but the truth is that we can start realising this utopia right at home and in our entourage. If each one of us started doing good deeds on a daily basis, alleviating the plight of our fellow humans, we would have islands of peace and love that could spread to become continents and even reach the four corners of the earth one day.

A new earth awaits us. It dwells in our hearts.

ELEVENTH RESOLUTION

I Shall Be Spiritual

"We are not human beings having a spiritual experience. We are spiritual beings having a human experience."
– Pierre Teilhard de Chardin

WHAT DOES IT mean to be spiritual? To be spiritual means to believe that the physical world, the world of senses, the realm of becoming, is pervaded by — and the product and manifestation of — a higher, subtler world — the world of Being —, and to live and experience that deeper dimension of being.

The world of forms is a materialisation of the world of ideas. However, unlike what most religions preach, the "other world" is not to be found in some unreachable "heaven" but within us; the Kingdom of God dwells in our hearts, as Christ said. Matter is made up of dense energy and lower vibrations, matter is spirit taking form. Nature and the universe are the body of God, the manifestation of Pure Spirit on the material plane. The universe is God's body, and we humans are His soul.

The consequence of such a spiritual world-view on the human level can be summed up by the following axiom from the Vedas: *"what a man thinks, that he becomes."* Man's whole intellectual makeup and his whole life are reflections of his thoughts, his state of mind, which determines his actions and behaviour. Thus, a noble, lofty soul will lead a creative, spiritual life; a base, vulgar soul will lead a parasitic life of depravity and lust. A free spirit

will uplift life and his fellow men, whereas a lower soul will live in the chains of matter and be plagued by suffering.

Why is it important to be spiritual? And how does one become spiritual? Being spiritual means that, without neglecting the outer, physical world, we nurture our inner life and feed our souls, focusing on the essential and the eternal aspect of existence: the spirit. Everything else fades away with death; the spirit alone remains. Therefore, it is futile to cling to the transient and the ephemeral, to our possessions and our status, for, at the moment of death, we are all naked, destitute. *Everything we have, we are bound to lose one day. What we are, however, we shall always be.*

The only thing that remains after our physical demise is the love and good deeds that we have bestowed on our fellow humans on this earth. The real, eternal you is not your perishable ego but your immortal soul.

You should therefore identify with the boundless within you lest you live in vain and die in pain and regret. View life as an opportunity to love and to grow, to create and to experience *Ananda,* the "Joy of Being." *To be, not to have: that — in a nutshell — is what being spiritual means.* This is important because by focusing on the real essence and purpose of life, which is none other than the divinisation of the human, and the humanisation of the divine, we fulfil our divine potential and our divine destiny. To be means to love and bless life and all living creatures, and to be blessed by life; to have is to lust, to crave, which leads to suffering, envy, division, greed, hatred.

Spirituality, the higher, enlightened faith of free spirits, is the "third way" between crude religiosity and atheist materialism. But it is first and foremost a practice, not just a set of beliefs. *Spirituality is a way of life;* it is the way to live the Divine Life

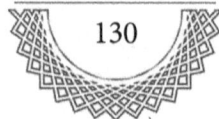

on this earth, to achieve heaven in the here and now. The atheist believes in no god; the religious believes in the transcendent god; the spiritual believes in the Inner God, in the God-Man. Therefore, the divine is only known and experienced by the spiritual person as a Son of God.

In our material world, there is a perpetual war surreptitiously raging between hostile egos who lust and crave instead of loving and longing. The sad fact is that most of us are ruled by our egos. Egos separate and divide, whereas the souls commune and unite with each other and with the world, even as the cells of a body work in concert to sustain the life of the organism, and cancerous cells develop when they break away and disconnect from the whole.

Modern life is focused on having, instead of being and giving. *"You are what you have"*: that is the rule today. Our possessions, our status, our bank account, the fancy clothes we wear, our luxury car: that is what defines us. We frantically accumulate riches and thereby grow poorer in spirit. Our inner life is poor or even non-existent. Universal love remains a utopia.

Thus, the materialistic vision of the world holds full sway today. The outer, material world is the only reality that we recognise and live. Few people: philosophers, thinkers, poets, spiritual masters, artists... have an inner life. Most of us are purely outward-oriented; our souls — which are our inner depths, our true nature — remain unknown to us. We remain strangers to ourselves. We identify ourselves with our perishable ego instead of our eternal self or soul.

Materialism breeds nothing but poverty of mind and death of soul. When we judge things, people and life itself from the materialistic viewpoint, we breed fear, greed, hatred, violence, injustice, and all sorts of suffering.

Yet the truth is that there is another dimension to the world, and that dimension is spiritual, the realm of the spirit, a subtler realm transcending all things material. Spirit moulds form and shapes matter. *As within, so without.* Spirit is omnipresent, it imbues the world with life and creative evolution.

By living on the spiritual level of existence, one attains inner and outer peace and harmony, as each soul develops and bestows the human virtues of love and compassion (which, as I said before, are also divine virtues), and, thus uplifting itself as well as life, becomes self-realised and fulfils its full potential. Consequently, justice is upheld and safeguarded, talent and merit are expressed and fulfilled, and love rules all.

Spirituality links the world of forms with the world of ideas in an organic unity. In order to be spiritual, one has to put the material in the service of the spiritual and realise that the material world is but a manifestation of spiritual forces at work — and our thoughts are part of these spiritual forces — and this spiritual energy that pervades the universe seeks to express itself in the magnificence of life and eternal creation.

My formula for being spiritual is the following axiom by the great psychologist and mystic Carl Gustav Jung:

"The Soul Is The Only Reality."

The soul is our only real and eternal identity. Beyond the material world lies a deeper, wider reality. Our inner life is a world unto its own, it is with our thoughts that we create our destiny; the outer world is shaped by our thoughts and feelings. It is when both the inner world of ideas and the outer world of forms unite that we become whole and realise our human as well as our divine potential and vocation. "(Real) *ecstasy is the*

liberation of the mind from its finite consciousness, becoming one and identified with the infinite," wrote Plotinus; that, in other words, is what Hindus call *Samadhi* — union with the divine —, a state that is reached by the very few initiates.

I — and more precisely, my soul, the eternal in me — have borrowed this body in this life in order to live, feel, create, but I am not this body, or rather, I am *not only* this body; I am much more than this body. My soul is a ray of the divine Sun, of the Universal Spirit. I am eternal and infinite, beyond identities. I was never born and will never die, for *that which is unborn cannot die.* I am the Spirit manifested in human form. I am in God and God is in me. That is the spiritual vision of the world.

When one acquires this certitude and adopts this attitude in life, the impact is directly felt within and without, within and between souls. Awakening occurs, awakening to a higher, deeper dimension, to the essence of existence. Petty worries and shallow differences between men fade away in the light of this truth, in the light of Truth. Thus we fulfil ourselves and live according to nature, to our true spiritual nature. Conflict subsides, there is unity, all becomes one.

Realising our true, higher, spiritual nature leads to spiritual growth, healthy relationships based on empathy, compassion and brotherhood. Man thus overcomes his human limitations, fears, lust for and attachment to material things, and becomes divine, "perfect as his Father in heaven is perfect." And in this harmony and perfection the tree of happiness can take root and bloom.

TWELFTH RESOLUTION

I Shall Revere Life And Its Mysteries

"May my soul bloom in love for all existence."
– Rudolf Steiner

"**N**EVER WAIT FOR *a miracle to believe in God. Your existence is already a miracle."* Life is a miracle, a daily miracle. Every single minute of every single day, a miracle takes place in the mineral, animal, human worlds and in the cosmos, and that miracle is life itself: the birth and the rebirth of plants, animals, humans, countless stars and galaxies. *The miracle of creation and perpetual evolution,* the beauty and perfect order and harmony that characterise nature and the universe, the infinity and eternity of Being and Becoming, all these miracles surround us humans, and yet most of us are so engrossed in our petty worries, concerns, ambitions, etc... that we fail to admire all that perfection and beauty around us.

One need only gaze at the countless stars on a clear summer night to feel totally mesmerised by that divine beauty and to wonder about life's great and eternally unsolved riddles and unfathomable mysteries. A divine vertigo overwhelms us when we view the world *sub specie aeternitatis,* from the viewpoint of eternity, instead of from our small, narrow earthly lives. When we gaze at the starry night sky, we feel in total communion with the Cosmos. *We behold the face of God and feel His heavenly breath in the depths of our souls.*

Life is a gift and a blessing; it is definitely worth living, despite illness, old age, death, suffering... for these woes are counterbalanced by the joy of being, the innocence of youth,

the beauty of nature, and the blessing of love. There are miracles every day and everywhere, beauty surrounds us and love blesses our hearts; and yet, somehow, most of us fail to wonder about the mystery of life and fail to see all that beauty around us, focusing instead on our insignificant worries and narrow ambitions. Most of us remain impervious to the mystery of creation and blind to the divine Light that sustains life on this earth and in the universe.

Why is that? Why don't we appreciate life and feel grateful just to be alive and glad to experience life's daily miracles? Most of us only see the half-empty cup; we complain about what we do not have and fail to appreciate life's many joys and blessings. The reason behind this negative attitude lies in the fact that we do not see ourselves as agents of creation, as co-creators involved in life's grand scheme; instead, we view ourselves as separate, "independent" or "unencumbered" egos and become the prisoners of our social roles and petty materialistic ambitions. Thus the beauty, the magnificence and mystery of life elude us and we remain trapped in the insignificance and evanescence of everyday life.

The result of such a narrow materialistic vision of life is suffering, frustration, sorrow, anger, envy, disappointment, tension and violence. Instead of being a symphony of love and a manifestation of divine beauty and perfection, Life becomes an unpleasant and painful burden.

What, then, should be our attitude towards Life? We should learn to *experience life as a daily miracle.* Mysteries abound around us; we should learn to perceive, recognise and admire nature's beauty and its many wonders. Thus we realise that we are the Sons of Creation, united with Life's very soul and purpose, and we start living in accordance with nature's eternal,

divine laws which elevate and glorify life. We become divine beings having a human experience, and human beings having a divine experience.

How is life experienced as a daily miracle? Many are life's mysteries, many are life's blessings, but love stands apart as the greatest blessing of all. Love is a divine gift, the most divine of human feelings; it alone makes life worth living. Everything else fades and dies, but the power of love is truly the greatest miracle that fills our lives with the joy of being and the bliss of eternity. Therefore, we should know, experience, and bestow only love, love for our soul-mate and sweetheart, love for our family, friends, fellow humans and the entire universe.

My formula for peace and happiness:

"Live To Love, Only Then Will You Love To Live."

(The Epic of Arya – In Search of the Sacred Light).

Love all and everything. Love the sunrise and the starry night sky; love the mountains and the valleys; love the kindred souls that bring joy into your heart; love everything and everyone that makes life worth living.

We should practice reverence for life by devoting a moment each day (it could be half an hour or an hour if we have time) meditating on the wonders behind creation, whether on earth or in the universe, thus filling our hearts with love, love and gratitude for life.

When admiring a lovely sunset on your own, ask yourself the perennial questions that pertain to the essence and meaning of life: *"whence did we come? Why are we here? Whither are we*

going?" Think about the mysteries of life: the mystery of birth, creation, the mystery behind the universe, the meaning of existence... *situate yourself as a witness — and even as a co-creator — in this daily miracle that is life.* Say to yourself: *"I am a Son of Life, the meaning of my life is intimately connected to the meaning of Life, as everything is one. I should awaken the divine in me, as eternal creation and elevation characterise life; God is eternally becoming, expanding, creating and recreating Himself and the universe. I am a part of this cosmic dance. Through love, I am human; through love, I am divine."*

By beaming divine and healing rays of the light of love, we express our gratitude for our blessings, the blessing of life and its beauty and magnificence, the blessing of love... and we sink into awe and wonder before the mysteries of the universe. By relishing the inner silence, we awaken the divine in us which is intimately linked to the divine in nature. We become one with God.

Develop awe and reverence for life, the universe and creation, for the mysteries of life.

What is the impact, on us and on those around us, of such reverence for life? *If you smile at Life, She smiles back at you.* Thus we become connected to the Whole, the eternal and the essential, and we ignore and transcend our little worries and annoyances which then seem like specks of dust in the infinity of the cosmos. Life becomes imbued with magic and the Joy of Being blesses our heart and soul. We talk to God, we feel his divine breath and hear his divine symphony.

HEAVEN ON EARTH:
THE SECRET OF HAPPINESS

THE DESIRE TO be happy, the search for happiness, is a natural, inborn human instinct and longing. We are all programmed to seek happiness and avoid pain. Happiness is our ultimate goal in life, our holy grail: *"and then he saw that Brahman was Joy; for from Joy all beings have come, by Joy they all live, and unto Joy they all return"* (Taittiriya Upanishad).

However, throughout the ages, we have forgotten how to be happy, we have unlearned happiness, because we have lost touch with our inner nature, our true nature: our soul. It is in the soul that joy finds its home and its fulfilment. But our souls are atrophied in this world of obsessive consumerism and frantic accumulation. The world has become too complex and too complicated, thus we have lost the simplicity and innocence of being, we have severed our link with Mother Nature, our link with our own soul.

The soul in its purest, unaltered form is a sanctuary of peace, serenity and bliss, for it is connected to and part of the Soul of the World, the Breath of God. The ego, on the other hand, is the source of all our woes and suffering, since it thrives on separating, dividing, grabbing, craving, lusting for petty material pleasures and ambitions. When it becomes an end in

itself, when it ceases to be the instrument of the soul, the ego becomes a source of suffering and an agent of destruction.

Therefore, in order to rediscover happiness, we should revive our souls by reconnecting with life's true meaning and purpose: perpetual creation and eternal self-overcoming. We are on this earth not just to enjoy ourselves but also — and more so — to fulfil ourselves, to reach our highest intellectual, spiritual, moral potential. The meaning of life is not happiness but fulfilment. Or rather, *true happiness is self-fulfilment*, not evanescent pleasures. *True happiness is a life of meaning;* and the highest meaning is the soul's liberation and elevation, the divinisation of the human, and the humanisation of the divine.

So long as we are not in touch with the Soul of Life, our souls will remain empty and lost. By reconnecting with our inner self, with the divine that dwells in our very soul, we reach inner peace and harmony, and fulfil our highest potential. This self-fulfilment brings joy and meaning to our lives.

As I have demonstrated throughout this book, happiness is a conscious decision and attitude, a way of life; it is a state of mind that transpires in a constant, daily practice. Life could be filled with joy and meaning, or it could be the antechamber of death, a sea of heartache and regrets. It is a question of perspective, of how we view life and death, and our *attitude* towards life and death. Do we view life from the perspective of death, or death from the perspective of life? It is all a question of perception and attitude. We ourselves create our own destiny, we ourselves decide to be happy or miserable, depending on whether we adopt a positive or negative outlook on life, people, events, etc...

However, as I said above, we have unlearned *how* to be happy. We have forgotten the simplicity and innocence which are the essence of happiness. The rampant materialism of our times

has rendered us captives of our status, our image, and locked in a constant struggle for survival and domination, nearly completely stifling our longing for spiritual self-realisation and elevation, as we struggle to survive in a merciless world of tension, competition and conflict.

Only by reversing this trend and living a rich, full spiritual life can we hope to rediscover happiness. Spirituality makes us focus on the essential, seeking the light in everything and everyone, instead of being possessed by our possessions and obsessed by success and greed. Thus happiness becomes a natural reflex and way of life.

The twelve simple but important resolutions that have been put forth in this manual of happiness are intended to help us better deal with life's trials and tribulations, to let us take control of our life and to make the best out of it, by adopting a healthy, positive, life-affirming attitude and state of mind at all times and against all odds.

Some readers might wonder why none of these resolutions is specifically about love. The truth is that love is the essence of happiness, happiness is impossible without love, and the twelve resolutions that I have shared with the world are all imbued with love, they all recommend adopting a loving attitude towards life and towards our fellow humans. Love and self-fulfilment: these are the twin pillars of happiness which the twelve resolutions that I have put forth strive to attain.

Love is the essence of happiness. And yet *the highest love is love of the highest,* love of perfection, which is the manifestation of the divine on earth. Wikipedia defines *Arete,* the Greek word, as follows: *"in its basic sense, means excellence of any kind. In its earliest appearance in Greek, this notion of excellence was ultimately bound up with the notion of fulfilment of purpose or*

function: the act of living up to one's full potential. Sometimes translated as 'virtue,' the word actually means something closer to 'being the best you can be,' or 'reaching your highest human potential'."

Arete: this is what true happiness is all about; self-fulfilment, which of course is impossible without love, love of oneself, love of life, and love of mankind at large.

This is my recipe for happiness. I hope the readers will try it, enjoy it, benefit from it and share it with their friends and loved ones in order to make our world a better place to live in.

ABOUT THE AUTHOR

Ambassador, Philosopher, Scholar, Author, Poet.

Dr. Taha Audi holds a PHD in Philosophy from the Sorbonne University, Paris, and a Master's degree in Political Science from the American University. A senior career diplomat, she has previously served in Geneva, Paris, and Tokyo, and was appointed Consul General in New York in 2019. In addition to her diplomatic and academic careers, Dr Audi is also an internationally published author of several books, translated into several languages, and numerous articles, in the fields of Philosophy, Spirituality, Politics, Poetry, and Literature, as well as several works on International Law and Organizations, most of which were adopted as official documents by the UN. Versed in philosophy and mysticism, the author espouses a spiritual worldview and believes that man's ultimate purpose and vocation in life is the fulfilment of his divine nature and destiny. Dr Taha speaks fluent English, French, and German.

Some books published by the author:

- Rousseau, le dernier bon sauvage, ou l'âme de la République ("Rousseau, the Last Good Savage, or the Soul of the Republic") (Dr Taha's PHD Thesis, to be published soon).
- *Fallen Suns, Rising Stars* – A Novel about Second Chances (Literary Talents, Amazon, USA, 2019).
- *Twelve Resolutions for a Happy Life* – A Manual of Happiness (Manticore Press, Australia, 2015).
- *Verses of Light* (Arktos, London, 2014).
- *Defining Terrorism: The End of Double Standards – Towards a universal definition of terrorism* (Arktos, London, 2014). The book was translated into Portuguese and published in Brazil.
- *The Epic of Arya – In Search of the Sacred Light* (Author House, USA, 2009; second edition: Arktos, London, 2016).
- *Nietzsche, Prophet of Nazism: The Cult of the Superman* (Author House, USA, 2005). The book was translated into Portuguese and published in Brazil.
- *Le Dieu à Venir de Nietzsche, ou la Rédemption du Divin* (Editions Connaissances et Savoirs, Paris, 2005). The book was translated into English under the title *Nietzsche's Coming God, or the Redemption of the Divine*, and published by Arktos in London in 2013. It was also translated into Spanish.

Facebook page: https://www.facebook.com/Ambassador-Dr-Abir-TahaAuthor-236100370816

www.ingramcontent.com/pod-product-compliance
Lightning Source LLC
Chambersburg PA
CBHW022026090426
42739CB00006BA/299